EZIZWENI

EZIZWENI

UNTOLD STORIES OF AN ANCIENT AFRICAN CIVILIZATION

THABO CLIVE MATHONSI

REBEL SATORI PRESS

New Orleans & New York

Published in the United States of America by
Rebel Satori Imprint
www.rebelsatoripress.com

Book design: Sven Davisson

Paperback ISBN: 978-1-60864-256-4
Ebook ISBN: 978-1-60864-257-1

DEDICATION

To the WORLD that didn't dub AFRICA when
she asked to be heard from the backrow!

Chapter 1

Ekuqaleni (In the Beginning)

Before the desert winds carried any heat and Tshaka was labelled the African Hitler, there was a man that resembled the true epitome of evil and his name was Kane. History and geographical citations tried to erode this traumatic legacy of a man who even the great Samouri Toure said he was like a blizzard that only blew to signal victorious tantrums! Born as the only bastard son of King Menelick, of the Bhanda kingdom, he was an outcast and even worse, an albino! His father was an old fool who had unimpressive imperial ambitions compared to his greed for concubines and slavery. Therefore Rah, his army commander, a well-oiled battle machine that never lost a one on one fight, plotted a coup to dethrone the indolent king.

It was called the 'coup de *Bacayi*' meaning the expulsion of the weak one and Rah together with Prince Theodore the 3rd, [the king's second born son] were the catalysts to this incident. King Menelick always kept a close council of old women and men that had served his father before he died called '*Abavuyo*'. This council was tantamount to the existence and steadiness of the entire Kingdom in reality, because the King viewed and believed their advice to be directly from the ancestors and former Kings of the Bhanda clan. Hence he feasted and even kept leftovers of every advice they gave him, despite that there was a chieftain council that should have been the focal of all state and legislative affairs.

There was a large atmosphere of discontent and persistent need for fresh air and blood on the throne and Rah knew this very well. He knew that out of all King Menelick's sons, Theodore the 3rd was the most ambitious and cunning. Everything related to power, politics and war was very much appealing to him, his elder brother used to nickname him 'ihlosi elingelamabala'[1] signifying his wayward character and unusual ambitions and nature compared to others.

Rah with a few noble and respected chiefs held a meeting nicodemously with Theodore the 3rd, to convince and feed his unquenchable desire for power. The plan was simple. At the feast of green leaves, which was the annual banquet before people could began harvesting, King Menelick would be merry, relaxed and drunk from the evening's lavish and extravagant activities. Normally the royal guard "Imbazo" would be secretly drinking also as it took shifts to guard the royal house. Therefore for a proper assassination to take place, this was the ideal and most favourable time if ever their plan was to succeed. So they waited and acted calm until the rains ended.

Kane at this time was labelled as the white devil sent by the King's enemies from the underworld. No one wanted to even hold him and love him. Even his own mother died of shock when the midwives showed her the 'taboo' she had brought into the world! She was beheaded after her death and buried headless in the common graveyard of the damned called "abathakathi." This meant that Kane was doomed to die before he even suckled his mother's milk and sat on her bosom. Nevertheless as fate would have it, Glenda an evil and powerful witch from the *Kahut* tribe picked him up at the *Ngalade* River's mouth before the waterfall.

1   Spotless cheater

She had heard visions of a white warrior that had a large birthmark on his back in the shape of an assegai.

In her dream, the warrior was powerful so much that even the crocodiles of *Ngalade's* calmer waters escorted him along the shore in a straight line. Glenda knew this was a sign from the ancestors and gods of water so she went early to bath first at *Ngalade's* shallow and deep end. This was the part of the river that had all the herbs and disposed material that she needed to perform her trade to the highest quality, and most people were afraid of this therefore it became a witch's convent and place of peace.

Just as she was pondering on her vision, she heard a baby crying. She knew that her vision was true so she waited for the river current to push the baby to her and so it did until she could see it up close. When the straw like basket floating vessel was near her, Glenda hooked it with her *"ntonga[2]."* It was him!" The warrior she saw in her visions, pale, white and unusual from the other human beings she had ever seen all her life. He had the mark she was looking for. It was obvious from his eyes that this child had a story to tell and show. So Glenda took him to her house near the *"abathakathi"* graveyard! She was an outcast also as she was labelled an evil witch when human flesh and blood was found in her *"qhaga"* by her relatives during a family event. She was banished from the local community and her right eye, middle fingers and big toes were amputated as part of the punishment for her trade.

This incident made her bitter and outright evil because she had been sabotaged by her step brother Maliq who was a powerful wizard himself. Maliq wanted to take Glenda as a wife as custom would have allowed it since they were not real blood but Glenda was unfortunately

---

2   A wooden rod that has a hook at the end/tip.

given to another man as wife who was richer and more able. This didn't sit well with Maliq, therefore he went to the jungle and conjoured up a powerful concoction and evil enchantment that whosoever passed through the biggest Baobab tree of the Makhambe jungle would be devoured by hyenas.

So it happened that Glenda's husband was that person since their house was the nearest to that jungle and he loved the Mopane tree that was very good for firewood near it. The hyenas dismembered him horrifyingly, blood was all over, but his head and family emblem beads that everyone wore around their neck were left. Maliq knew that his work had the results he wanted. If Glenda didn't want him nor did his family want to give her to him then no one was going to have her he thought. Hence he took the head of Glenda's husband and grinded it with *imbokodo*[3] until it was pure mincemeat. He then took that and poured it into iqhaga which he then planted at Glenda's house during her mourning period This is how Glenda the good became Glenda *umloyi*[4] and from that day on she vowed to get even and to eat her enemies flesh for the rest of her life.

This Kane was a child of her enemy, a king who banished her and shamed her in front of everyone. Her revenge was going to be sweet she smiled. Surely he was going to be a delicacy since he was white meat and was unusual from the common flesh she was used to thus a big meal needed proper preparation. Glenda went too look for spices she had farmed around her place and oil from the pig's loins that she had gotten from a customer as payment for her services.

3   A big stone
4   The evil one

4

"This is going to be epic and a real banquet to remember," she thought as she scratched her dirty hair with long crackly finger nails. Then as the water she had placed to boil the boy was at the favourable temperature, the same vision she had seen before came back to her but this time it seemed too real and severe that it left her shaking and with a headache. Therefore she begged for forgiveness and mercy from the ancestors and looked for goat\cow mixed milk to feed the boy. Since the boy's mother was dead she was his mother now, a second chance for her to have a child she always wanted and to teach the child her own will. So the boy grew, strong, pale and full of soars at first because of lack of knowledge about his skin and condition but eventually Glenda knew how to treat his condition.

Back at the royal house, at the dawn of the feast of green leaves. The coup was ready to take place and so was death to feed upon another royal's blood. Theodore was going to do it personally and Rah was going to send and lead *Imbazo* away to get more wine for the king's quarters whilst telling *iSgubudu* the royal brothel to keep the king company. The *iSgubudu* was one of King Menelick's grave weaknesses, especially for the foreign concubine of the 'Hakira' clan, the pony tail people called Willow.

Willow came to the Bhanda kingdom as a captive after her people were defeated by Rah's ruthless army and her father was stoned to death for refusing to openly kneel before king Menelick. She was young at the time but she realised that to survive as an outsider she had to quickly align herself with powerful people or else she would suffer the usual fate of slavery and frequent abuse from her captors. So she found herself at the king's private chambers regularly because she was completely different and wise. The first day the king saw her after they had been numbered to serve as slaves at the king's farm, he quickly told the young Theodore the 3rd to hurry and bring the girl to him.

He instructed him to tell the *Mpashi* to not mark her for she had found favour from the King. The young prince went hastily to do his father's will but when he was up close about a metre away from the slave girl's sight, he understood perfectly why his father wanted her. She had the beauty and presence of a person that knew her worth although deep down she had the heart and blood of a stone cold killer. Young girls at her clan were trained profoundly in the art of assassination and patience using *ifohloza*. Willow was one of the best in this trade and she knew that there was nothing like fortune and love in life but only power and death.

It was part of her initiative to make sure the old king sees her as she had frequented where he was time and time again from the slave brander's quarters and the king was hooked. What she didn't anticipate was the young Prince's interests also. From a bird's eye view, Theodore the 3rd was the tallest and most handsome warrior in the entire kingdom. He was about 8 feet 2 and had the strength of two infuriated grizzly bears. At one point he domesticated a leopard as a sign of his unchallenged strength and prestige but the cat disobeyed him one day. It ate from his 'umganu'[5] and he punched it once and broke its jaw as punishment and that story served to add more upon his outstanding prestige.

So being overwhelmed was an unknown thing to the young Prince especially for a giant that stood over and shadowed everyone. Willow was different, in all the kingdom the young Prince had never seen such a beauty before. It was like a Romeo and Juliet love at first sight kind of experience but only this time, Romeo was the only one in love! Words

5   Wooden plate

ran away from the young Prince as he tried to address the slave girl but he finally mastered the words to tell her.

Theodore the 3rd: The green eyed beauty from the clan that sleeps and eats upon a knife's edge!

Willow: The young Prince that sees everyone's front and back from afar! Tell me my lord, what I am thinking right now? (Giggles a little)

Theodore the 3rd: Let's see! Hmm! you are acunning and naughty one, so you are thinking of ways to remove those shekels on your hands and feet aren't you young lady? (Grinning)

Willow: True young king, um impressed, the rumours are true, you are wise and clever beyond the known and unknown indeed!

Theodore the 3rd: (smiling slightly) Rumours are wielded by sharp tongues and broken mouths beware of the vessels who spread such doom and baggage of lies!

Willow: "Hail to the greatest warrior in the Bhanda Kingdom!"

Crowd: "Hail hail hail hail Theodore!"

To this, the young Prince was amused and very happy about, since his ego meant everything to him and here was everyone aiming to over-feed it with praises! He liked the slave girl instantly and she seemed to like him back, at least he thought! But then again the king's will over-comes feelings and desires, and the young Prince knew very well that his father was merciless when it came to women and any threat to his affections towards them. Therefore he quickly relieved Willow from her bounds and led her to the king's royal quarters.

King Menelick didn't waste any time as he quickly ordered the *aba-gezisi* (to bath and pamper Willow with the best ointments and herbs, to make her as beautiful and attractive as possible. They did this with haste and when they were done they presented the new reincarnated Willow to the king in his private chambers and he almost suffered a stroke with shock and lust! It had been long since a woman made him feel like that, it was like his first time seeing a girl, Theodore's mother before she died an abnormal death.

Queen Zimaa was her name and she was beautiful but unfortu-nately she died at an early age of 33 after giving birth to Theodore the 3rd! The midwives said it was because she didn't have enough power to push the baby so they had to cut her open to save the king's son but in reality, the lack of civilization and education at the time claimed a lot of souls because of their misguided methods. So the king lost the love of his life due to the carelessness of the 'clever' midwives but Willow had a presence about her that ignited a weird spark deep down in his broken soul. She was young and about the prince's age but she was royal trea-sure now and the king's servant to use and abuse at his will. Therefore king Menelick kept her close as his favourite concubine and periodic supervisor and therapist for some time.

On the other hand, the young Prince hated this because he also wanted the girl to himself, and the girl confused him even more because she would sometimes sneak out to have a quiet and private time with him *egangeni*[6]. She was playing both father and son's feelings and yes, she was winning! The prince began to be disrespectful and to second guess his father's judgements and acts whilst his father sank in deep in *'monopolized love'* with the slave girl. So when Rah had first approached the prince about the coup, at first he rebuked Rah and threatened to tell his elder brother Nazaar who was next in line to be king but as time went by he began to hate his father.

As his anger intensified, he sought Rah and the chiefs in an act to construct the cinematic plan that turned a tide and shook the Bhanda kingdom! Willow was to be used in this plan and she gave her full support because she was tired of the company of the grey dreadlocked nymphomaniac king. The plan was simple, Rah had already done his part therefore, Willow had to make sure the king was in the royal common room *'ehontshini,'* where she was to keep him company together with other concubines until the young prince entered the room.

Rah had given her *umvagasi* poison nto spike the king's beer before he drank it and, she managed to do that easily by letting the king enjoy the company of the other women whilst she claimed to go and refresh and bring more beer for all of them. The purpose of this poison was to make sure that there was no witness when the King was assassinated. It was the type of poison that literally ate human flesh from inside-out within seconds and it was appropriate in order to kill every concubine that was with the king. However the antidote for it was simple *'ubisi lwehotshi'*[7] and Willow knew this well. In order for her to be safe from being blamed for the assassination, she also had to take the poison but

6   A secluded and hidden rocky and bushy area.
7   Warthog milk.

the young prince would hastily come to her aid after killing his father.

So Willow spiked *umgqala wonke*.[8] She contemplated on what she was about to do as she took slow and dragged steps back to the room full of fools that didn't know that she was literally the devil's advocate, death itself, the eater of worlds. They all drank in their heightened spirits of joy and coughed out the red wine that begs and proposes for death to get in, blood! The sight was truly painful because the first symptoms were blindness and swelling of the stomach, then the feet and hands would also jump-castle into extreme expansion as the veins and arteries explode internally.

For the weak, death came quick and easy, it was like they wouldn't even feel it but for the strong it was the worst way to die and for a king it was unspeakable. One by one the concubines died screaming and scratching each other as they blindly sought for the locked door. No one was near enough to hear their screams or at least give them closure as they slowly withered away in pain. The gods and ancestors they prayed to had forsaken them, one of them lamented as she took her last breath. Blood was all over the place, 'iskhumba senkosi[9] was almost soaked to its natural wet state because of the pool of blood all over the floor.

Even *icansi*[10] looked like uncooked macaroni rolls in a red tsunami of a soup, with blood all over. However the saddest part was the sudden bang on the door. The young Prince stood at *umgubazi womnyango*[11] caring the royal ivory and gold short handled assegai with a large and

8   The whole beer gourd

9   The royal animal skin carpet

10 A grass made like mat used as a bed

11 In Africa, strong poles used to support doors

double tipped diamond spearhead that couldn't break nor be scratched despite the countless bones and lives it had come across, as it claimed countless "rebel souls" at King Menelick's hands.

It was his turn to feel the irony of the idiom that says *'zibanjwa ngezikudlayo*[12] and King Menelick loved women and power, something that his son wanted more than anything and yes, enough to kill anyone for it!

So as his father was lamenting in pain and about to go fully blind, the King heard large footsteps and saw a shadow that was not of an ordinary man. He smiled in his pain as he coughed out what seemed like chunks of meat and blood.

He knew it could only be his boy, the giant prince, his most beloved son, the only reminder of his true love, Zimaa, his seed and rescue. He tried to smile with his blood covered beard. However the Prince was crying and holding his father's assegai as he locked eye ball to eye ball with his father.

King Menelick: Help me son, I am dying, its cold and it hurts!

Theodore the 3rd: All I ever wanted in life was for you to recognize and love me more as a son but you never did and always blamed me for my mother's death. I wish I can help you Father but this kingdom would continue to suffer. I love you: *Ncwelibazi, Ngalade, Sidleke Samabovu, khanka lase nkangala, Mdlalose kazulu, Matshutshu kaBhanda, umaZidla zibuthene Kalanga, Khathaza sgingci sikaDlodlo,lala*

12   Foes are overpowered through their strengths and what they love most

ngokuhle Nkosi yam, Mahluleli wam, baba ...(sob-
bing and screaming in pain)

The young Prince stabbed his father straight in the heart to finish him off and relieve him of the pains of the clutches of death. As King Menelick took his last breath he kept saying *"iyeza inkawu"* and this was confusing to the young Prince. Although his feelings were mixed, he cried heavily for his father. His father might have been a monster some-times but he was still his blood and he felt deeply gutted for what he had done but this job wasn't for the weak.

He knew the job wasn't done yet because he had to give the wart-hog milk he came with to Willow as fast as possible or she was going to die also. All this time she had managed to hang by a thread due to the little warthog milk she had sipped before taking the poison. The fact that the milk was in her system, was what kept her alive to that very moment. So the poison took longer to affect her as compared to the other victims.

Theodore quickly gave her weak and lifeless body huge gulps of the milk and she woke up after sometime like a super charged and cranked generator. She was alive and the plan had succeeded for now, the Prince thought. But then again the biggest problem was his elder brother now, the new king if culture was to be followed, therefore it was time for phase two of the grand plan.

Nazaar the 'dark one' was the immediate heir to the Bhanda throne. His great grand uncle from his mother's side, chief Tuku of the Tarrasa ruins nicknamed him the dark one not because of his unnatural level of melanin pigmentation but because he was the only person that he ever saw kill a buffalo and stand to tell the tale. He like general Rah was made for war and even 5 wizards and 5 witches died whilst prophesying about the birth of a dark champion of the Bhanda kingdom.

Their nails and eyes shockingly turning a deep dark black.When he was younger, King Menelick was still in his youthful years, energetic and determined, would teach him things that only a nemesis would wish to do to its worst foe. He called it preparation but in reality it was child abuse at its worst though that was unknown during those times. For every training duel Nazaar got stabbed or injured by his sparring partner, the King would cut and carve his failure and the name of his victor's name on his back until he mastered to be the best and kill all his sparring partners.

For every kill, his father slew the biggest male lion to signify his greatness as a supreme in the art of war and they would both eat the heart of the lion raw and paint the tombs of the fallen victims of Nazaar's *mkhumbane* with the lion's blood. He was the face of hell if it was ever to be personified through a human being, and his angry demeanour didn't help either. He was known to bed at least 4 women a day because of his abuse of the *umdledle* tree that had dry roots that were grinded into powder to intensify and boost the libido of the royals so that their genealogies would be guaranteed through siring many children.

Unfortunately, he was infertile and this made him more intense and evil towards most people especially the commoners. At first, women were killed and fed to the crocodiles for not giving him the children that he desired very much. He would first stab them in the stomach with a ritual knife used for male circumcision rituals called "*ivala-vula*." He would then curse their ancestors and their weakness in giving him a weakling of a wife or concubine as he spit in their blood stained stomach.

That instance, their insides would shoot out blood and unpleasant human secretions. After that he would throw them into the river. Therefore king Menelick devised a plan to help make his son happy and whole again. Young Prince Theodore was a teenager by that time but already a huge man by stature and by all means fertile. The King bound the young Theodore to a secret child siring traditional custom that is aimed to aid an infertile family member to get children through one of their blood family members and the tradition was called *ukulamuzisa*.

So it came to pass that whoever Nazaar took as a wife, young Theodore would also sleep with them, to save them and sire children for his brother and for a time. Nazaar became happy again and his demeanour changed as he began to love and understand the world again. But then again the murder of his father was a sudden shock for him as much as everyone else.

"How could someone dare try that knowing what he would do to them if he found them?"

He screamed to the earth as he tore his remnant and cried for his father. He couldn't piece how it happened but he knew this was a huge political coup and plan devised by powerful people in the kingdom, people like general Rah, he thought. Naazar never liked general Rah because he thought he was too ambitious and driven to play second fiddle to anyone. There he was bound to be treacherous sooner or later and he was right. However, he hated that people always compared their similarity in stature, demeanour, fighting technics and ruthlessness. They were both merciless and shrewd battle tacticians although Rah was older and theoretically wiser.

Nazaar knew he couldnot trust anyone from the royal council but only his brother Prince Theodore the 3rd and other family members, as the news had come like this, that his young brother and father had been attacked in the royal chambers by an unknown group of local assassins called *Omangenakuvaliwe*[13]. These were known to use every weapon and supernatural means possible to kill whoever they sought to kill, as Theodore had survived with a few wounds and a concubine.

Theodore had made sure that in order for the final phase of the coup to be truly effective, Rah had to dodge the royal guide at a certain grape vine. That was a segregatory place for the blind, because the place was deemed too dark to tilt, and the grapes too dark and bitter to eat, therefore only the blind could live in the area.

It was more of an execution in a way because the blind never survived for long, they would munch on the grapes for some time until they would die of eventual, thirst, malnutrition and animal threats. The royal guard was a different ball game, however Rah knew them all well as he had trained them. He knew these were men of war and stone-cold killers that would do whatever was necessary even if it meant death for the crown.

Soto avoid any survivors to tell the tale of the coup, every possible alibi, link and witness of the coup had to die. It was painful walking with his 'sons' as he called every soldier to their death which he was to be guilty of. It washowever necessary evil that would foresee a better future for the kingdom he thought.

When they got near to the vineyard he told them to go inside the mushroom mountain, where the physicians usually gathered some of their needed insects and organisms for medicine. It is common knowledge that mushrooms usually attracts all types of living organisms.

Inside, they were to look for *omangenakuvaliwe* as the man-made

---

13   Best army unit in the land

Intel had proclaimed them to be there and so the royal guard went inside in stealth mode and very alert. Rah had managed to pay some few local huntsmen to gather for him about 4 chariots full of all the poisonous snakes available in the kingdom. They brought him 5 because everywhere they went searching for them they found a plethora.

So they had littered all the snakes inside the cave the previous day. The snakes were by now agitated and aggressive. Two of the huntsmen had died whilst offloading them due to the snake bites but their money was sent to their families, as Rah was indeed a man of his word, if it suited him. The plan was to close the cave as soon as the entire royal guard was inside, so that the snakes would feast on the evidence as he thought. So as soon as they were inside, Rah rolled a large stone with the help of some of the huntsmen's that he had paid. The huntsmen sneaked out of the bush and from their stations for this final part of Rah's plan and the cave's mouth was closed.

From the strongest to the wisest, the snakes left no stone unturned. The royal guard crumbled at the might of the slithering reptiles as it was not geared for a challenge like that. For the people listening outside, there was a classic orchestra of screams, hisses and curses as the soldiers took some of the snakes out and they also got painfully bitten, again and again. Rah knew it was done, so after 30mins of waiting for the dead silence, the mountain was quiet and calm again. Only the smell of dead bodies and snakes dominated the place. No one was left standing and even the snakes were totally decimated despite their deadly poisonous bites.

It was a bitter sweet story of a hunter that got hunted and died with the prey, sad indeed! Rah on the hand, knew this was exactly going to plan and disposing the evidence was going to be much easier as he piled the dead bodies, with the help of the huntsmen inside the mountain. Then he beheaded all the dead snakes and made a circle of their heads, around the piled corpses of the royal guards. He then broke all their spearheads and stabbed them all with them in the heart as a sign of honour and respect. It was believed that a man carries his worth to the afterlife through the tip of his spear and is allowed to the ancestral realm if he carries his 'mantle' and marker of greatness to appease the gods.

This was goodbye Rah sobbed deeply. Some of these men saw him as their own father but he had condemned them to their doom for a future that was uncertain. He however knew that the snake heads would guide and protect them against evil spirits that could afflict them on their way to the afterlife, even though he knew it was a setup to blame this incident as an act of murder and evil exorcism and treason by "Omangenakuvaliwe."

People knew that these assailants were known to engage into s witchcraft acts and they were swift hand to hand combat killers. They were masters of the dark arts and illusions that knew how to and when to appear to kill and disappear. Since they were a group of outcasts and abnormal, their strength lay in being fast and disappearing before they were caught.

Their leader was Tahia, a giant multiple limped woman who had the shadow of a spider showing off its 8 legs from afar. She was born a taboo at birth as she had an extra limp for almost every part of her body. Instead of two hands she had 4 hands and an extra finger on each hand and she had strong and big feet that couldn't fit in the traditional

"Sengilisi"[14] that people wore at the time. Her throw was the best in the entire world. At one time she let a victim run away and when they were about 120 metres away, she threw *umkhonto*[15] and hit the victim. It pierced through his neck and pinned him to the near Mopane tree as his blood cascaded to the ground to form dark earthworms.

This is believed to be the reason why amacimbi began to flood and evolve on the Mopane tree. That was a seasonal reminder of the day Tahia killed a foreign gladiator and pinned him to the *Mopane* tree. In hand to hand combat she was unstoppable. She could hold the enemy with her hands and kill with other hands, and there was nothing they could do about it. Her close friends called her umaNkala because of her crab like stature. Others were abnormal too. Some were born with no feet at all and some were lepers, down syndromes, deaf and rebels. It was easy to notice that these people had talents that could break the scope and scale of capabilities and abilities.

In the Bhanda kindom, being different or behaving differently classified one as abnormal and disabled, and the usual verdict was death or absolute segregation from the entire land. This therefore meant *Omangenakuvaliwe* was a safe haven that harboured everyone despite their differences. It was more than a group, it was a community, a world to feel free and embrace one's uniqueness. The royals hated that because these people who they were indirectly condemning to death were living and multiplying in numbers.

When Rah returned to the capital, he blew the rhino horn to signify an imminent meeting and attack on the capital. Naazar was busy seeking answers from his young brother about what had happened to

14 Sandal

15 In Africa, isiNdebele term for a Spear

him and their father, when he heard the kingdom's roll call. He wondered what this meant but he knew he had to hastily go and see and evaluate the situation as the new king. Rah being a marvellous orator began the final piece of the puzzle and greatest speech of his life.

General Rah: Dear beloved people, today is a tragic day for our kingdom! An enemy lives amongst us, a beast has manifested its fangs and clawed our children in our midst whilst we were pouring and touring our land in love and unity. Someone in this great nation has brought evil upon us children of the iron kings. It is sad that I merely escaped whilst my brothers were butchered by these assailants that have pestered this kingdom for years. Yuri of house Vaala is dead, Ronan of Anspa, dead, Tar of Venin, dead! All of them are dead! My brothers! (*sobbing heavily*). How long shall we stand and conquer nations after nations when the real enemy lives amongst us and continues to plot scheme and rob us of our loved ones? How much more shall we cry and keep on burying the dead after celebrations? I swear unto you brethren and dear sisters! Hear me today! It will be my life's work to dedicate myself to find *Omangenakuvaliwe*" so that they pay for what they have been doing to us as a nation!

Crowd: Hail! Hail! Hail, General Rah! (*Clapping, shouting and rallying behind the speeach*)

19

Nazaar:	Quiet! (*dead silence*), Indeed today has been a grievous day for this nation as there is even bigger and worse news! The king is dead! (*Cries, moaning and noise erupts*) He was murdered by someone in this place right now! General Rah we are very happy that you managed to survive the attack from our enemies and that you are safe to lead and galvanize the kingdom's army again. As the new king, I promise you that this incident will not go unpunished. Whoever is found guilty amongst you, I swear to kill you personally and very slowly! The burial preparations and mourning procedures are to begin right away and general Rah is to tend to his injuries! Dismiss!
Crowd:	*Bayethe Nkosi, Bayethe nkaba kaBhanda Bayethe!*[16]

As they walk away mourning and crying for the dead king as custom required them to *ukuzila(upholding strict mourning norms)*.

Nazaar knew he had to play it cool in order to get on top of this situation therefore he acted dumb. In the coming days he listened to Rah's lies as he narrated how it had all occurred. What he failed to understand was why he had to go personally with the royal guard or at least deploy the *Nkisela* as they were known to always deliver. On that same day, he had lost a father and his best friend, Yuri who served as a captain in the royal guard. . It was politically orchestrated but impos-

16 African totems

sible to prove. All the chiefs that were involved in the coup had sworn a blood oath to keep this secret and take it to their grave.

Theodore had fully recovered in a week and so had Rah and Willow and it was nearing the1st day of the week, which was the day for burying kings.

Nazaar and Theodore were both wearing the royal mourning pangolin skin encroached gown that had porcupine spikes at the shoulders. A lion's mane topped the collar and a zebra's skin flowing downwards. It was all threaded together using the hair from a hippo's whiskers. The entire population, was in the traditional black kilts made from a speckled black goat skin and all of them carried the burning elephant tusk as a sign of respect and brightening the path to the afterlife for the great king. It was a custom that had stood for years and the burning horn as they called it, was sacred.

For every Royal member who passed on, it was set ablaze but this meant that eventually the elephant tusk would burn up to ashes inevitable. None wanted their horn to burn up the fastest because it would mean automatic selection and death, since the royal were accompanied to death. From the old to the youngest, necks were broken and the corpses were piled chronologically in terms of age, power and rank. The body of the royal was supposed to be surrounded and protected and nourished even in the next life.

Animals were also slaughtered and the villages would drink their blood and then spit on the ground.

This was also doneto the big and wide grave with countless dead bodies of humans and animals and wild fruits. This was done to signify and acknowledge the late king's power as a leader and true blood that had sovereignty over all the land, game and people even at the afterlife. The royal house had to take a hand full of ash and salt and pour it all over and around the late king's body until it was totally covered. This was a way to discern and showcase the difference and position of the king compared to the commoners.

It was a personal and heart felt way of a family to say goodbye to a father, brother, husband, grandfather and leader. No commoner was supposed to touch the king's body, only his sons were allowed to. His wives were the ones who were in charge of washing him and soaking banana leaves which they had to wipe his whole body with. This was a sign of eternal service to the crown and king even after death. His daughters were in charge of gathering bees and wasp that was to be used for the fattening process. It was simple, the king's body had to have the biggest and noticeable body form all the corpses, especially because his was in the centre

Therefore to perform such a miracle, the bees and wasp were poured and trapped around his body in their thousands until they had stung him to their death. This would in turn soar and expand his already big frame to almost double or triple his natural size. This would make him an outstanding site for the gods in the afterlife. This was however the first process before the royals poured ash and salt upon him.

Finally, the whole kingdom would take a handfull of clay soil and one by one they would pour it ontop of the corpses surrounding the king's body until they were fully covered. The royals would then pour gold and silver fragments on top of the king's body and finally, pit sand on top. His sons would then have to carry a big stone around the burial site and carry it around for 10 cycles around the burial site singing and praising their father. This was a way of appeasing and appealing to the ancestors to welcome the king to their realm.

Finally, the stone was set on top of the grave and his assegai was laid on top of the rock. His wives had to sleep around the grave for the night and his daughters had to bring food continually until day break whilst the sons had to look at the moon until it went down. This was the final phase of the burial process and the final goodbye to a great king. The people were dismissed after the grave was full covered in soil and only the family was left to finish the burial processes.

After the burial, there was supposed to be two weeks of silence and zeal before a new king was appointed but at present, the kingdom was divided as to whom should inherit the throne. By right, Naazar was the rightful heir to the throne but most commoners had never forgotten his yester evil antics and actions towards them. Theodore on the other hand was young and driven but very much the sweetheart of the kingdom.

Rah knew it would only be a matter of time before Nazaar figured out what had happened therefore he sought to speed up the final act of the coup. He assembled all the tribal chiefs and philosophers. His question simple yet very treacherous and pure treason!

General Rah: Fellow chiefs, wise-men, scribes and seers we are gathered here again to deliberate on the future of this great kingdom. A kingdom without a leader is vulnerable to its enemies and my friends we have a lot of them. Nazaar is the rightful heir to the throne as we are all aware but as this oak tree that we are gathered under is to bear witness. We have all heard the rumours and rumbling from the midst and all walks of life from this kingdom. Dare I say that I know what you are all thinking

23

great ones but we can't avoid the possibility of the signs and rumours of being right. We all loved king Menelick but the truth is that he lost his way along the way and the kingdom suffered in result. Shall we ignore the signs if they show and point to a better way forward, a peaceful Bhanda state, more food and wealth to the chiefs? Dear brothers, I see a choice and a way and Theodore the 3rd is that way!

Chief Zubah: As the voice of this senate, I hear you dear brother and I am glad someone had the guts to raise this issue before it spilled over in an unjust and bad way. However Nazaar is the rightful heir to the throne and any thoughts or acts towards challenging that is an act of treason that should be punished by death. Yes! Menelick was a great king who made mistakes like those before him but let it not be forgotten that under him, this kingdom managed to defeat most of its foes due to his greatness and military prowess that Naazar also has in abundance. Naazar is a hard and intense man but he is exactly what every kingdom needs in order to survive in this "treacherous and wicked" world. I say Nazaar is the best and rightful way forward.

Chief Uro: This meeting on its on is treason to the crown and I fear it might be a problem for all of us in the future as we all know that Nazaar neither forgives nor forgets! I agree with Chief Zubah but we have already failed to honour and respect Nazaar by agreeing to meet and deliberate about the state of affairs that we shouldn't deliberate about in reality. My brothers! I fear that we are all doomed for death unless we choose Theodore!

Chief Fei: I am a man of honour and respect, my allegiance will forever be to the rightful heir and therefore I will bow down to Nazaar alone.

General Rah: *(Seeing that there is a big division on this issue and that some chiefs might betray him, as he had foresaw and was told by the sorcerers, Rah ordered his loyal soldiers and chiefs to kill all those that favoured-Nazaar)* Is there anyone else that sees Nazaar as the rightful king? Perfect! We are all in agreement now brothers therefore we have to kill Naazar today whilst his heart is still fond and mind still tender from losing his father! The plan is very easy, we are going to go and see him in *"Emadwaleni ezansi"*[17] where he has sojourned since the burial to complete the 2 weeks of silence and mourning before he becomes king. I am going to take my trusted faction of *iNkisela* and we are all going to go with your tribal armies to attack him and

17   Rocks of the South, a peaceful and desolate place of ruins that was full of rocks.

kill him there quietly with his other brothers and family members!

Deep in the rocky areas of the south, Nazaar had a bad dream! He saw a crab fighting with the desert wind and the wind turned into millions of tiny sand desert termites. The crab tried its best to fight and kill some of its attackers but it's every snap and kill was returned and countered by rapid termite bites! In its last breath, the crab tried one last feat to escape and as fate would have it, a large army of nocturnal and strange insects flooded the plain and picked of the termites one by one but the biggest of them escaped. Naazar woke up afraid and confused early in the morning but his brother Amien had a gift of foresight and explaining dreams. He knew what his big brother had seen and was wide awake before he was.

Amien: I saw it too brother and yes the desert storm is coming and blood will be spilt but it is not your time yet great king!

Nazaar: What does it mean half-brother? Is someone amongst us going to betray us or kill us? Their own blood and family?

Amien: It doesn't matter if we are already dead big brother, what matters is the choice you take from now on! Go with haste! The crab is waiting for you now! Go! But be careful not to be heard or seen brother for some of your ancestors seek to do you ill and condemn you in blood to this bewitched

26

land! A woman you shall seek and a woman shall you see, but be swift and steady and don't question your thoughts for you shall be the victor over your enemies, and they shall bow before you. Now go brother, your journey has begun my King!

Nazaar was confused and afraid, from what his brother had just proclaimed, he was herding for doom. He had always trusted his wise advice and knowledge as they were about the same age but of different months and mothers. They were not of equal rank despite being royals but Amien respected honour and drive in a man as his brother had, and Nazaar was a fan of intellect and wisdom which Amien possessed. This meant they always respected and accepted each other better than others. In his dream, the crab was in a war at the plain of Nova, a wellknown arena for gladiator sports and illegal combating betting. It was a fight to the death type of sport that demanded insanity and pure adrenaline to take in properly.

Every minute, a warrior fell and the ground devoured and quenched it's never ending thirst for more lives and blood and the crowd loved it! Nazaar was aware that in these lands, he was just like any other man and this made him vulnerable if ever he was caught snooping around. People at the south were savages and wore and acted differently but they could identify well with one another. An intruder was welcomed with spices and knives to the throat to fend of other clans and tribes from spying the land and the territory.

This was Tahia's territory and here she reigned as queen. However an invasion from a stronger foe that had a unique and sublime art of war that the entire Bhanda kindom nor other kingdoms had ever witnessed had rendered her weak as she was defeated in the battle of Yok! She and her army of abnormal assailants *Omangenakuvaliwe* had suffered their first ever defeat and failure and it was a grave one.

The rumour was that they came from the north but what was true is that this new race of invaders was ruthless and well-oiled in war. They moved with one purpose, stride and action .They were not muscular people or big bodied compared to the *giants* in the Bhanda clan, and other surrounding kingdoms but they were swift and had weapons that were made to knock down even the toughest of the warriors in Africa, as Tahia had found.

When they fought at Yok, Tahia was sure of a win as the enemy had sent a mock army that had weaklings, scared and untrained soldiers in it. However this was part of the plan as the mock army was the bait for Tahia's army so that the invaders would pick them off easily, one by one. The mock army was a group of initiates that was deemed too weak to fully grasp the hardships of being a man, and war and was usually drafted from men who were infertile, lanky and physically disadvantaged. Their tongues were cut off as punishment and encouragement for them to work harder to be like other warriors and men.

For those that absolutely failed, the outcome was to gain honour by dying for the cause of your kingdom as bait that the commanders saw fit! In this case, death was the honourable service to the cause and the mock army would take it in style as they would run at the enemy like a well-oiled battle machine, only to be killed in numbers. This, however meant that Tahia's army was exposed in its full capacity at the centre of the plain of Yok and the enemy was fully ready for them.

They called it the bow and arrow and the double edged sword of Yamakha, weapons made from the morning dew of the lands of their ancestors they said! Against the traditional assegai and hand to hand combat, these weapons were a miracle reborn and fabricated to totally outmatch any opponent. The northern men had surrounded Tahia and her army and the rain of arrows fell hard on them! Thousands died and fell and for the few that were left to fight the enemy had a surprise for them.

This was the real birth of the long animal skinned and wood platted battle shield that had iron hook at the tip of each end to injure enemies and tore their flesh in close combat. With the sword and shield, the assegai was no match for such an event and so the *Omangenakuvaliwe* fell and Tahia was badlly injured together with some of her fellow warriors. The northern men had conquered the Bhanda kingdom's most hated foe single handed.

Tahia had lost one of her hands, although it was still functioning. The war had broken her but she was strong despite that. Her people needed her the most now although she stood as a shadow of her former self in terms of confidence, doubt and belief. They were now slaves of the northern men and entertainment at the arena. They loved her the most because she was the best gladiator they had ever seen, and because of her abnormality she was just perfect for the sport.

For her, every fight meant that she had to kill one of her brothers and sisters, and it tore her apart every time she won, to the amusement of the gibberish northern accents of the northern men as they joyed and placed bets on the next fights! Who could help her, she always cried alone at night at the prison cells that were made from the toughest bamboo and gum-tree poles!

The prison was impossible to penetrate because it had a self-killing and triggering mechanism that made it suicidal to every prisoner. A rope was tied to all legs and hands to sharp bamboo rods that were organised in a circular way to compress every time the rope stretched as the prisoner tried to move! It was like million needles compressing towards someone every time they took a deep breath or moved too much, it was the epitome of prison life at its highest point!

Nazaar had arrived at the time when the northern men were away for a raid and had left a few people to guide the slaves. Due to greed and the love for the arena, the guards, casted lots and the gladiators began the common blood bath to the death with the new weapons they were not accustomed to fight with but they wielded them better than their makers! Just as Nazaar was watching in hiding behind some rocks, he heard a big cheer emanating from the camp as a big shadow of a crab graced the sands of the arena's floor. It was like the best feeling and moment he had ever had and seen.

The crab in his dream was actually a giantess and warrior like he was. She had battle marks and scars like most accomplished heroes and heroines but to him this was what he had wanted all his life. In a glimpse, he pictured himself in love and happy with this woman and having many strong kids like they both were but reality settled in when he heard another huge cheer. This time he saw her fully from head to toe as she had just killed another gladiator whilst holding another against the wall.

She was beautiful and had a strong physique but possessed a feminine look to her muscularity that drove Nazaar crazy with desire. As she knelt on the ground to rub some mud on her hands as it was her custom after every kill. A sign of belief in the will of her ancestors and hope that they accept all of her opponent's fate, Nazaar was almost salivating at her sight. This was someone he could love truly, talk strategy with and spar with daily as a possible better sparring partner compared to the numerous ones he had killed.

The arena was again in full roar as Tahia won against everyone they set against her but as they were busy cheering her greatness in combat, Naazar had quickly managed to sneak inside the barracks. He had managed to stalk a drunk guard near the eastern side of the gate that had a watch tower made from assembling rocks together, until they reached a particular height that allowed the watchmen to see all over the place.

This however invention had many loopholes such as soil erosion and the need for ultimate concentration because it could be an anchor for enemies if the watchmen didn't do their job well, as the rocks allowed an attacker to run quickly or stalk them to death without being heard. Nazaar had managed to kill both watchmen with a small-pocket knife that was made for quick and close quarter stabbing called the *io-Kappu*.

Due to the noise at the arena, no one had heard him or the watchmen scream and squeal as they took their last gasp of breath. The chief captain of the barrack who had been left behind as the one in charge rose up and for once spoke to the slaves and all who were there to listen or partake.

Remeses the 1ˢᵗ: People of our great city and metropolis of the Nile, we are the true Africans. We are mighty in war, superior in arms and ahead in change! To those that still wonder because we look different and wear elegantly through and through even in war. We are not the enemy, we are merely your salvation and only window to the future! You are all pigs and barbarians that dance for straw of the northern men as you have termed us! But we go by a different name, race and age. We are the chosen race to bring retribution in this ungodly and impure land full of evil. Don't worry, only the strong of you will live and bath in our sympathy and glory like our champion 'Serqet' (Tahia) "*(named after the scorpion Egyptian goddess)*. We are the Egyptians, dwellers of the Nile and kings of all Africa! Cheers brothers! (*Taking a sip of the marula wine and gurgling it and spitting it on Tahia's face*). Ain't she wonderful? My own champion and ugly queen of the sands! (*All Egyptians laughs except the slaves and Nazaar who was over boiling with anger in silent hiding.*) Prisoners! I dare you today, if one of you has the guts to truly live and be free, please stand up and face our champion! If you kill her then you are free but if she defeats you, I will feed your carcass, bone by bone to the hyenas of my Commander Ahmmed Tetris!

Crowd: (*There is a dead silence as everyone is looking at each other but knows that they don't stand a chance against Tahia but suddenly a deep voice with authority and charge echoes through the entire place*)

Nazaar: I will fight her!

Remeses the 1ˢᵗ: Who are you slave? I have never seen another big one before except her? Where do you come from dark one? Ooh! I know you are the last of the Rundi tribe that we killed along the river near the gorge of Komodo, those were some dark ones wherein they brothers? (*The Egyptians laugh and agree in union*). Tell you what dark one? You kill her and I will pardon the fact that you miraculously showed up and make you my champion! It's a deal right? Guard! Give this man a weapon, I am sure he will need it against the scorpion queen! Let the games begin!

Tahia was quick to attack as usual as she wanted to finish the fight as quick as possible because she was ashamed of how the drunk captain of the barrack had treated her for sport and amusement of his own people. She didn't care that this new opponent looked over dressed and strange for combat because Nazaar had worn a torn kilt of a dead gladiator from the western tribesmen of San. The kilt looked over sized and unpleasant because it had sucked in blood and water for a long time, and had expanded as it was made from a rare combination of animal skin hide that expanded due to too much liquid exposure.

Nazaar was also quick to jab away and fend off the attack with the unusual weapon they had given him. He was the master of the assegai, no one could stand against him when he was using that weapon, but because his late father was a weirdo and a lover of all things pain inflicting, he made sure Nazaar was also a master of stick fighting. A sword to him wasn't as much of a big deal as some had made it to be with their lack of diligence in mastering it.

He knew he could kill Tahia with one move because he had watched her fight before and saw all her vulnerabilities, but he wasn't here to kill her. He now fully understood his dream, he was the help to the crab that was attacked by the desert wind and termites. He fully understood that these termites were fools of their own amusement hence he had to dance to their tune for a while and give them a show to remember.

The crowd was on fire seeing Tahia attack and Nazaar fend her away like master teaching his student. Some of the slaves were beginning to ask themselves who this new challenger really was as they had never seen someone totally outclass their queen in hand to hand combat. Whoever he was, Nazaar had managed to use the hairs of an ox tail to disguise himself to look as hairy as possible, a trick that Amien had taught him when they were little and playing hide and seek to confuse and fool their friends.

It was time he thought, therefore he moved closer to Tahia and quickly hit her hard with the blunt centre part of the shield on the head and she fell headfirst into the sand. Nazaar went on to stomp her tenderly but theatrically with his legs to the ground much to the cheers of the arena. Deep within, he knew he had little time before his disguise fell off and his plan would fail. So he got on top of her and acted like he was about to choke her to death and whispered to her!

Nazaar: For being my foe, you fight very well strange one! But face it, you have lost beautiful! Let me make a deal with you and I promise to spare your life.

Tahia: All this time I have wondered how I will die for all the lives I have taken, and if it is by your hand then I receive my destiny, I die with honour at the hands of a warrior who bested me in combat! But because you are a man and a man thinks his winning every time he sits and stands on top of a woman, you have lost sight of my greatest

34

strengths. Tahia uses her upper hands to choke Nazaar and inverses her hold using her strong legs and lower hands to get on top of him choking him with force and purpose, grinning with an evil grin of finally being on top of her opponent.

(Drooling a little blood from her battle bruises on the mouth) Tell me now handsome, who's on top of the world now?

Nazaar: Wait, please stop! I am King Naazar of the Bhanda kingdom and I am here to set all of you free my queen!

Tahia: You are no king! You are just a strong chunky fool that knows how to fight better that everyone I have ever faced in combat!

Nazaar: Check the necklace! The emblem and gold totem on it, I had a dream that I should come and save you from these evil northern men and I believe we can take them out of we attack them together and we free your people!

Tahia: Here we are, with the king, at my mercy, both as slaves and you are talking about dreams and possibilities! What if we can't make it out and we both die as fools and slaves? What then? What future will there be my king?

Nazaar:	Your stubbornness amuses me in very complex ways but we both know it's the right thing to do and by now they know who I am because my fake goatee has fallen! Rise with haste and fight with me, here they come!

As Naazar and Tahia were busy exchanging chokes and opinions, Nazaar's top front of the kilt had fell off exposing the strongest built and muscular back that the whole of the Egyptians and the gladiators had ever seen. It was like the fat dark man from before had transformed into a war tank and lord of war! Everyone was shocked, it was an illusion but they were more shocked when he turned over and they finally saw the dark man without the fake goatee and it was the future king of the Bhanda kingdom, Nazaar the ruthless himself!

With haste, Nazaar and Tahia were up and ready for the fight of their lives. Their differences and opinions wouldn't matter if they couldn't live long enough to tell the tale of their current and pressing predicament. It was truly one for all and all for one as the "great musketeers" greatly put it. The Egyptians as they called themselves where of different built and school of thought compared to the other parts of Africa. Wisdom was born and bred from them and civilization was a toy they drove daily in the muddy and paddy plains of Africa, as they conquered and indoctrinated many states, using both brutal force and a peace by choice mechanism that they called necessary imperialism.

It was simple, bend the knee and submit to their rule and lifestyle or die where you stand with your 'stubborn and underdeveloped mind.' There was no time to convince a stubborn man, he or she had to submit to his or her master instantly as a sign of respect after defeat or face the inevitable death that most famously chose with great pride. In their military training, they were groomed in totality of understanding an enemy's weakness and strengths. This was their greatest strength more than anything because they never dared to attack someone or people they knew could outmatch them or probably kill them all. Nazaar and Tahia were both ruthless killing machines, they understood one thing and one thing only, revenge is best served cold!

The Egyptians were many and their pride was beamingly plenty. It was obvious that they were physically outmatched but they made up for that in terms of numbers. Remeses the 1st, ordered for their immediate surrender but Nazaar and Tahia spit on the ground and threw dust at them, as a sign of disgust and disrespect as was the *intimidatory* custom of the Bhanda kingdom's fighting culture. Remeses took this very personally since he was a radical and unorthodox Egyptian who believed that all Egyptians were born to rule and to be masters.

He ordered the famous and undisputed Egyptian champion, Razvan the 'long hair' to kill them all. Now this was a young man who was already a legend amongst his people. It didn't matter how big, fast or strong you are, Razvan could kill anyone without even taking 5 steps towards their shadow. He had the curse of 'Hithra' the Gold Egyptian god of war that had one weakness only, himself. Razvan was esteemed as a man of average height and physique like most people but beneath his Armour and over stretched smile lay a disability that made him the first ever double bone-marowed human being.

He had more bone content than human flesh and at times he would break his sparring partner's ribs easily without even feeling it because he would have thought that he had thrown a weak and friendly training punch. When going to combat, he only took his long battle fork-end knife and two black stones that his father gave him when he was sacri-

37

ficed in the ceremony of *Ceres*[18] He didn't need a shield because no one had ever survived long enough to even cut him or his long hair that was famous.

Tahia had seen him once butchering his Egyptian brothers that had stolen the general's mutton and it was quite a site. She knew very well how dangerous this foe was and she was scared. Naazar was also an undisputed champion of the Bhanda kingdom and ruthless as he was named. He feared no one and believed he was as indestructible as his father had taught and anointed him. With Tahia he had taken it lightly because he liked her and she was a woman, despite her physical frame, therefore he had toned down his fighting ability.

With Razvan however, this was a real man's game, a fight to the death that both men were ready for. Remeses the 1st was a firm believer and fan of his champion but for once his actions had caught up to him. The local marula brew that they were drinking the previous night had normal side effects for any normal person. They had grave outcomes for a typical man like Razvan. It made him weaker and slower than his usual self and this was a weakness that was very unfortunate against a warrior like Nazaar. As Razvan strode towards Nazaar and Tahia, he was blinded sighted by the sun's reflection from one of the weapons that the prison dogs were barking and playing over.

This was the birth of the common idiom,*"you slip, you blues"* that was later modified to you *'snooze you lose'* as Razvan's fate was sealed with one slip of sight and step. Nazaar was swift and steady with an assegai and his aim was unmatched. Just as Razvan was blind sighted

---

18 Ceremony of appeasing the gods through self sacrifice for a top seat with the gods and Pharoahs in the afterlife.

and... rubbing his eyes to see properly, Naazar threw his assegai and it connected deeply in Razvan's neck. That was the only body part that his bone structure couldn't help him and he died choking in his own blood, still holding his two black stones.

The victory birds surely were circling around Nazaar's courts because this was a shattering and shocking triumph to the Egyptians. Remeses the 1st felt it, they all did, the fear, the reality, the possibility and yes the reckoning of a possible death was nigh. Standing before them where two brutal giants, one unbeatable and the other formidable and special, they stood no chance despite their numbers. The other slaves were chanting and praising their leader Tahia and the soon to be King, Nazaar.

The whole place was in uproar and vibrated as they were also stomping the ground and shaking the jail gates. Remeses wished that the army hadn't gone out for raids because then, they would have been guaranteed of victory and at worst their life. So he tried one last trick to get on top of the situation by telling his man to put down their weapons. He said he wanted to have a harmonious and diplomatic understanding with Tahia and Naazar, something he called peace and democracy. He was mistaken unfortunately, as a savage understands only one language and rule, kill or be killed and Remeses was in range for his judgment.

Tahia hated him so much for all the mocking due to her disability and muscular physique. The time he would spit into the slave's food and urinate on them as punishment, if ever he was moody over his personal stuff. She loathed him deeply, and there was no turning back, no retreat and definitely no surrender but only death. As Remeses was in his philosophic and advocate persona, trying to get to an understanding with them, Tahia was counting his steps as she was ready for his tenth step near them. She was getting ready to behead him with the rusty and long sword that he had given her to undermine and disadvantage her in combat, in the arena the first day she and her people were captured.

Remeses the 1st: Where I come from, when an enemy is defeated and understands it through acknowledging in surrender, the victor spares them and sets them apart as message barriers or part of the clan. Surely we can assist the great and mighty king Nazaar the ruthless, the unbeatable one, king of kings and lord of lords. We are here at your mercy my king, as servants who now seek to serve and help in any way possible. As you know we are people of high intellect and technical brilliance, we can show and help this great land, people, children, army and King to be the best of the best and to produce the best weapons, ideas and innovations that this world has ever seen. Please spare us, spare my son, and spare my brothers and Ipromise to serve you all my days.

Naazar: You are right on one thing my friend, I need your kind for the scourge that is about to come. Since my father died, I have been betrayed and back-stabbed by those dear to my heart. Now look at me! A king without name, title and stake in his land because my very own blood brother seeks to kill me. I love him and always will but imagine how much of that has turned to raw hate. I willhelp you but I can't save you, I can only give you the assurance that every father seeks for their children and people, Iwill kill each and every one of you slowly and when I'm done, I will dissect your bodies and throw your ribs, one by one to your dogs that you love so much. (*Smiling devilishly*)

Remeses the 1st   Tahia please! Save us, I'm sorry, I am…

Just as he was pleading and begging for mercy, Tahia sliced his body in half with *insimbi edla ezinye*[19]. It was a clinch that Remeses the 1st was a victim of his own demise through the tossing of an iron that was forged to disadvantage the warrior in combat but Tahia had mastered all its disabilities and turned them to its strengths

During this process, the slaves had managed to break one of the prison cells and there was chanting all over as they attacked their captors with anything they could pick and throw.

Tahia: Kill them all brothers and sisters, take pride in victory that our ancestors have given to us today. We are better than these northern things. They tortured us, killed and re-killed us day in day out for fun and bets but alas today we leave no stone unturned, the only verdict is !vengeance Only live, Hadassah, Ada, Reba *hhahah*, Tutenhan and Sierra alive, for my king, for these are the wisest and beloved strategists and philosophers of the

19 A metal that destroys

Egyptians! As for Remeses' body, disassemble it, skin from bone and place his smelly skin as a flag on the gate of the garrison. Make sure his dogs eat his meat and finish it and then kill them too whilst their fullof it but do not touch his son, he is mine!

The slaves did according to their queen's bidding and Nazaar loved it all. The screams, bloody pools of his enemies as they hit the floor one by one and the skin-made scarecrow of Remeses the 1st's body on the gate, this was a sight that made him want Tahia even more and she wanted him back. She had never fought someone as strong as Nazaar and she knew that he could be the only possible man to live and to be able to tame her and keep her on her toes. After every Egyptian had been killed except the ones chosen, Nazaar talarmed Tahia to inform her people, so that they leave at once before the army found them. Tahia did as she was advised but she cut Reolon's (*Remeses the 1st's son and nephew to the Egyptian king through her mother, the kings' blood sister, Saraai who was married to Remeses the 1st and had been butchered also by Naazar and Tahia's people*) manhood.

This was an act of absolute disrespect and shame to the Egyptians and a clear message of war to the Egyptian king, Rathamon *the eater of worlds*, son of Rahim the sun god and queen Meza, goddess of the seas as he was known.

So they left, and took all the weapons, food and everything they would need for the journey back home and the megalomaniac war to come. Nazaar and his new found army, under the leadership of his crush queen Tahia, left for the plains where he had left his brother Amien and his other loyal family members. Nazaar had not anticipated finding such a sour sight for the living.

Everyone was dead, and their bodies were burnt!

The only remnants were their family jewellery due to their fire resistant qualities. General Rah had left them on purpose, so that Nazaar knew who was who in the ashy bodies of his loved ones. He was also sending a message that Rah was around! Nazaar wept. As the pain of the gravity of Rah's action sank in, Nazaar sobbed loudly. He had lost everything and everyone he cared about.

His newly found subjects bowed obeisance. It was custom that the king's tears received company, therefore everyone joined him in his lamentations until he was done. They dug up a huge gravesite and poured the ashes of the dead royal members inside. Since the disabled people were not regarded as people of any social class, they couldnot be sacrificed as accompanies to the afterlife for the deceased royals Nazaar had no sacrifices for his family. Naazar had to therefore cut himself and pour his blood into a sponge like bowl, they called *iwudlu*[20]. This was the royal seal the royals would need to be acknowledged in the afterlife, to be welcomed to the folds of their own people and cluster.

All the ash was poured inside the grave and Nazaar was the only one permitted to pour the ash traditionally. *Iwudlu* was smeared with blood and the deceased's ashes after which it was burnt, as a sign of unity and leadership to the afterlife. An element of their king, brother, son and sibling would be there with them even if he was still alive. And so, Nazaar buried them alone as he was the only royal alive amongst the living and Tahia and his people were forbidden by custom to touch or even think about partaking in a royal funeral.

It was time! Time for war, a time to decide and time to truly be king!

---

20   It was made from sheep skin and embroidered in pure white cotton.

Chapter 2

Imvukelo (War)

Rah and his Nkisela soldiers were ready and assembled. The message was simple, kill Nazaar and bring his head to Rah. Every soldier understood their duty to their *father of war* but they also understood how mighty their opponent was on a single one on one duel, therefore they had to gang on him to put him down. Rah's *izazi*[21] were back from scouting Nazaar's camp and they liked their odds against a weary, out-matched and out-numbered disabled army.

Rah knew to never think less of his opponent especially a ruthless man who had nothing to lose like Nazaar. Sometimes he secretly envied him and wished he was his own son, because he reminded him so much of his youthful days, , raw and direct to everything! So the battle custom began immediately as soon as *indosakusa*[22] had disappeared into the blue sky. It was called ukuza due to the fact that the greatest warrior gods and ancestors had to be appeased to come in favour and aid of whoever was conducting that activity.

Their presence was acknowledged in the levels of sound and battle war-cries that the army made as it disrespectfully swore on its enemy's ancestors' totems. To kill each and every one of their enemies brutally

21 Wiseman

22 bright and shinning star usually appearing early morning

44

and the large flame called 'uzulu'. This flame was every magician's dream, people believed and hoped on the trick before it was even performed.

Firstly, *inkuni zomkombe*[23] were gathered and then *amahlanga*[24] dry grass and dry leaves were assembled into one pile and set on fire. The real trick was hidden in the fire wood, as the red barky area burned away, it produced red like smoke. This was slowly followed by a large and abnormal burst of a big flame as the dark clot areamelted. When this clot melted, it became everything explosively dangerous which is why elders warn not play with when they is fire.

The fire transformed from camp and braai fire to a shocking red and hot glimpse of hell. It was a flame perceived miles and miles away. The belief was that this flame was a sign of presence and victory from the gods, so the people gobbled up this act like a hungry cavemen in a food factory. It was a necessary event in order to boost everyone's confidence and belief on the cause. Even the great Rah, loved this spectacle even though he knew it was fake as all generals before him did. It was an ordinary soldier's charm and spiritual relic to war but for generals it was a strategy to make sure everyone was ready for war. The general conducted this activity personally and banned the usage of this firewood for all basic activities except for this event in which he was the master of ceremony of.

"Yes, yes, yes!"

They chanted as the flame got bigger and bigger. Rah cut a piece of his beard and threw it in the flame and then everyone else followed suite. They then smeared their bodies with mud, and allowed it to dry for some time. Everyone would then wash it off and that water was used

23 Red barked firewood that usually had a dark hard clot in the middle
24 Dry maize, wheat and sorghum cobs.

to stop *uzulu* as it was believed to be the completion of the cleansing process before battle, and that the fire and land gods were with them in battle and in mind and soul. After that, everyone wore his armour, took their assegai, small stabbing knifing and battle axe with a sickle shape used to slice and dice an enemy and a medium-sized shield.

It was left for the general to tell his army to march towards their enemy's encampment and Rah did that without hesitation. The stomping of the Rah's army could be heard from afar as they marched and sang in harmony, to intimidate their enemy. Rah's army outnumbered Nazaar and Tahia's army with a clear 1 is to 5 ratio in soldiers and Rah's man were and true men of war, experienced and brutal compared to Nazaar and Tahia's army. It was a victory written in the heavens, Rah smiled as he led the march near the *Ziyankiyankiya* River. This was where Nazaar and Tahia, and their army, had resettled after the burial of Nazaar's family members. It was a strategic battle point especially because they had a secret weapon that even Rah, the battle tactician guru could not have thought about, the Egyptians!

To beat Rah, they needed a miracle and a half, it was like he was born to master strategy and he knew each and every move, before an enemy even thought of making it. The Egyptians were a new breed of challenge, they didn't conform to the normal norms of full on fighting battle tactics and strategies that were obvious to Rah. They were sly individuals who treated war as a sport, and they prepared for it with fun and assurance of seeing the next day.

Nazaar knew very well that his anger alone wasn't enough to guarantee victory, neither was his might and knowledge in war. If he engaged Rah's army directly, then they would have to face the possibilities of being butchered! He needed something new, something never seen, and something that would change the art of war, as it was known in the land. The 5 Egyptians he had taken as captive were the answer. They were the wisest people he had ever met and he had already learnt a plethora from them in a short while. More so than what he had learnt from philosophers in his land his whole life!

Everyone knew that Rah was the real deal, it was known but the Egyptians seemed to laugh about it and Nazaar almost killed them all in fury at their reluctance to map out the strategy to defeat Rah's army. They however quickly explained their reasons for being reluctant and it was something that Naazar had never heard or dared to dream of.

Sierra (the Egyptian):   For days you moaned great king and our condolences once again mighty king Nazaar but in that period we had already mapped out the strategy for this inevitable conflict with Rah. You see we are man of honesty and the truth is that you were going to lose and that was unavoidable! But you have a chance if you listen to each and every detail we give to you.

Nazaar: Speak on slave, I am listening…

Sierra: Go out and look for 300 fresh and long bamboo sticks. Tell the huntsman to gather 300 fresh animal skin that is strong enough to hold large stones and be not torn apart. They should also capture about 150 porcupines and the poisonous *girona* toad. Finally, great king, pray! For indeed you will need it!

Nazaar:	May I ask what all this will be for seeing that we are facing a war in a day or two from now north man!
Sierra:	Take haste my lord, take heed! Do these things now for there is no time to waste!

At that, Nazaar ordered all the relevant parties to execute those instructions and duties as Sierra the Egyptian had alluded. When everything had been gathered around, Sierra began to explain the grand plan.

Sierra:	You are great people, gifted individuals, people seen as weaklings in society but no wonder you know you are better than them! This is your fate, this is your destiny. Tomorrow can kill you, maybe some of you are already dead as your own gods have already highlighted in your few numbers compared to your enemy. But no man should die alone and live his enemy smiling over his corpse!

It rests on you to make the shift, the choice and have the vision of seeing another day, another laugh with your families, kids and wives! The plan is easy, they will come fast and hard, huffing and puffing their chests as they glide over the river to feed themselves upon you but that would be their biggest mistake. The river stream is shallow at this side of the plain, meaning that they can get to this side of the river bank easily but we want to kill them where they stand or at least where they wish to move and run to. All these porcupines shall be skinned and their spikes shall be poked on the *girona* toad. The spikes shall be cast under water and be held by a fisherman's net made from the strong bamboo skin. It shall be that when they attack and run into the water, they shall meet their fate as the poison kills in seconds and the spikes are very sharp. Eventually, they will put the dead bodies together and figure out a way of passing through unscathed by walking on top of them. Do not panic, it is within their right to come over and breach in our temporarydefence mechanism. Some of you are going to fall at this stage unfortunately but be brave people for that is the price of war.

Then at the sound of the king's horn we are going to run to the top of the cliff. It will look like we have sealed our fate as they will be no room or way to escape and Rah will know it. But we want him to think so, because he will send his army flying after us to the top but we will be ready for them at the gorge of the river's mouth. They will push us close to the waterfall and that's where we will use the bamboo sticks to roll over the big stones from the top, behind them. There will be only one way for them, death by stones or jumping over the gorge! But as for us we will use the cliff to our advantage as we know that there is an underground cave at the edge of the gorge that can be accessed by a rope and it leads to the other side of the plain. This is a result of the earthquake that took place in this area as we assessed. The animal skin, will be crucial for the young ones who make it to the end as winter is quickly approaching. (*Sierra looks at the king as if he also reads it that most of them will lose their lives and only a handful will survive but it is the only way if any of them are to survive at all.*)

So it was that everyone took point and executed the instruction. There was no war tradition in Nazaar's camp but just pure fear. They knew very well that things were beyond their capabilities, it was only a matter of fate and destiny and sheer luck for those who would live to tell the tale. Sierra preferred them exactlyas they were, afraid and alarmed. He knew very well that these were the very traits that most needed as encouragement to run for their lives when it was needed.

To Nazaar, it was a first time fighting against his own people and brothers. Some of them he grew up playing *laduma*[25] Tirza son of Rizler the blacksmith and Mila, born out of incest and nourished and molded out of pure evil, in the form of Rah, was a close friend of Nazaar. His parents had been ordained for death when they indulged in incestuous relations which was a serious taboo. Tirza was only spared by Rah who

---

25   a mud and stick sling game that is like an ancient version of paint ball using sticks and mud rather than paint ball guns

pleaded for him as a sign of victory and showcase of atonement from the blacksmith even after death.

That is why he was called Tirza, meaning the one who was atoned for in life and in the afterlife as Rah named him. He was also a formidable warrior who specialized in killing his rivals using a battle axe that he called *isinatha mazwe*[26]. He always saw a flaw in the assegai especially after it was thrown at someone and was evaded, that would leave a warrior open and vulnerable. His axe was made from a giraffe's hind legs and threaded through using the lion's mane. That was the lion he had killed the first time he held a weapon.

The head of the axe, was a remarkable thing in its own way. It was a big steel made and T-shaped axe-head, that was sharp and lethal enough to kill and squash two opponents in a single blow, that is if it was wielded by capable hands and indeed it was! For every kill, Tirza was blessed and cursed by choosing a female family member that was a virgin to take as wife. It was believed that the cycle and act of Rizler the blacksmith must be continued through his son. That would ensure that all weapons of the Bhanda kingdom would be distinct and flawless.

Since Rizler was the best blacksmith that the kingdom had ever had and through his blood and son, the kingdom was to continue being blessed to conjure the best weapons? So Tirza took many wives, sisters and nieces such that when he was walking with his whole family from afar, one couldn't see the surface of the ground because of the multitude of his family members. He was Rah's favourite soldier and indirect adopted son, Rah had taught him everything he knew, from how to hunt and how to fight but Nazaar had taught him how to survive!

Once, in their childhood days, an incident happened had which

26 Eater or drinker of worlds.

changed their lives. They got lost in a hilly area whilst playing hide and seek with their peers. The place was a den to a cult of amazimu[27]. The cannibals had seen them from afar of when they were giggling and running away from the one who was counting and quietly followed them to the hills. King Menelick had taught his son one special rule, that "*A jungle is never quiet when there are rivers that flow and enemies that seek and mockingbirds that beep!*"

Nazaar knew very well that something was fishy and off about the stillness in the jungle but he wasn't one to scare easily! He was a young boy at the time but he was a master in making traps and creating diversions. When they got near to where the cannibals resided they saw a gigantic steaming and boiling pot and a bonfire. Human skulls and bones lay in a huge towering pile and Tirza was scared but Nazaar knew it was their only window of making a run for it, before they were encircled by a group of man-eaters.

He picked one big and deformed bone that looked like a hammer with sharp ends and gave it to Tirza who understood immediately why he was given such a bone. It was similar to his axe! Then Nazaar picked two sharp bones at both ends and told Tirza to run towards the east. This was opposite to   where they were coming from, into further enemy territory. It was a huge call but it was better than being someone's supper! Tirza ran, he was a very athletic person and a speedy fellow but so was the appetite of the cannibals. They followed him relentlessly, throwing spears and assegais at him but he was clever to run in circles so he evaded their weapons.

Nazaar, meanwhile had hidden in the pile of bones. Although the cannibals knew that they were two potential *prey*, Tirza's burst and

27 Cannibals

strides in the woods had fuelled them to follow hard on him and forget the other party. The cult's leader had however stayed behind. His name was Moza and he was a giant ogre of a man. There were tales in the Bhanda kindom of savages and cannibals who were led by a monster of a man and Nazaar saw it firsthand. Moza was of similar height and physique with Theodore his younger brother, but he had bigger hands that allowed him to squash a human skull after he had drank from it.

Moza being a veteran and leader knew the other boy was around and nearby but he wasn't sure where until he had movements around the ruins of bones! He went running to check but was quickly met with an avalanche of bones as Nazaar had used two sharp bones to trigger an imbalance on the pile! It was such that whoever was close to the ruins would be buried by them. Moza was in pain and caught under the huge pile of bones but Nazaar quickly removed some of them such that Moza's head was left out in the open. Bruised, injured and trapped, the old fool had been trapped in his own back yard as the Ndebele idiom alludes "Zithiywa ngezikudlayo[28]". Moza wasn't angry nor hungry anymore but he was impressed. Out of every kill his cult had ever made, never had he ever seen himself being out maneuvered by a young boy. Tirza had managed to evade his pursuers but because the jungle was very tropical and marshy, he found himself back where they had been with Nazaar but this time with Nazaar and a trapped giant.

He was happy to see his friend and Moza was impressed the more to learn that the other boy also managed to evade the attack from his people. Tirza thought they should kill Moza before his people freed him. Their footsteps were getting closer and he didn't want to face them since they would obviously be agitated. Nazaar had other plans, he

28 Use what they love in order to catch them

wanted them to come and he intended for them to find this situation as it was.

He took a sharp bone and put it on Moza's exposed neck as he saw the raiding party coming. When the cannibals saw the two boys, their desire was fuelled! They were however forced to calm down when they saw their leader's head protruding from a huge mountainous pile of sharp bones. Moza ordered his people to stop and lay down their weapons for that day, they had been   defeated and outmatched by two boys.

He offered safe passage for them as long as they did not kill him. Nazaar however had a better idea, he made Moza and his people to make a blood oath with him. This was that they would never attack innocent people again but only feast on those that Nazaar or his father had condemned to death outside the land or to be hanged and in return the Cannibals were to pledge eternal loyalty to Nazaar in war whenever he needed them. Moza agreed to this and the place was called Mozambique to signify the Moza agreement/treaty. From that day Tirza knew that Nazaar was destined for greatness and he was a survivor.

Despite Rah not liking him when they grew up, Tirza always stayed true to his friend but this time, things were different, this was war and both of them were on different sides. Surely one of them was going to die but they both knew that it was every warrior's path either way to die for their beliefs and people, and they were ready for it at all costs!

The *Ziyankiyankiya* War

At the dawn of the month of June, Rah's army finally reached the *Ziyankiyankiya* River, after a two days march and the entire plateau was flooded with iNkisela! For those scared at the idea and sight of the face of death, this was too late for them. The Bhanda army was singing the common African mantra of,

"Liyabesaba na, hayi, asibesabi siyabafuna?" [29]

Back at Nazaar's camp, everyone had taken their battle positions, there was no time to waste but only blood to spill. The Egyptians had managed to make and attach a sharp blade and glove made from material on Tahia's amputated hand and she looked more fierce and powerful than ever. To her, these were the moments that legends were made from and she knew that her king and husband also understood this, as she had never kissed a man in all her life except Nazaar! They had made a pact, if they both survived this war, they would rule as king and queen together up to the end of the world. This was sealed by *isiqabulo sika-zulu* [30]. It wasn't a mere kiss between two lovebirds but it was beyond organic emotions and feelings.

It was a kiss that signified the birth of a new world and race of the Bhanda people, a union between royalty and outcasts, the birth of a group called *"Amahole* [31]*"* The union was however fated to be if they survived the war. All parties were happy about this union and it had come at the right time, because this gave the people reason to fight. They needed to matter finally, to be entitled and yes, to be a true Bhanda again!

29 Do you fear them, no we don't, we want them *meaning we want them dead*

30 Kiss of the people

31 Specially recognized low class royals (a major upgrade from being outcasts) NB: this was only going to stick if they survived the war.

As *umkhwezeli*[32] was signing a song titled, "*Vula masango singene*[33]" and Rah's army backedhim up with discord singing the chorus "*sithathe ukudla ukudla kwezitha*[34]" Nazaar threw a long spear at him which went through his mouth to the back of the head. This made Rah very angry as it evoked confidence and noise from Nazaar's, camp as they cheered at their leader's act. Rah immediately commanded his army to get into their battle formations. It was a simple battle formation, a leaflet from Alexander the Great's might in warfare.

Instead of the cow-horn formation that amazed Africa in the later years, Rah had developed a formation that he called *inyoka ezidlayo*[35] The idea was to not only encircle the opponent but to be fluid such that even when an enemy deflected to a certain point, in an attempt to expose weakness, , the formation would not allow it. The head, which is the strongest faction of the army would be at defense position, there-fore allowing the snake to grow another head that would then bite itself to close the weakness.

Further, it would encircle the opponent, squeezing tight at all ends and inside, such that it would be a game of shooting darts until all were killed or apprehended! This tactic usually worked well and efficiently in an open field but Nazaar knew how to maneuver in it and that is why he had chosen the *Ziyankiyankiya* River base, as the battle ground. He knew that Rah would have to break new ground and formation in or-der to defeat him and this was something he was betting on his former

32 A war singer and speaker who was chosen for his outstanding theatrics and war motivational slogans and songs

33 Open the gates so that we enter

34 So that we take our enemy's food

35 A snake that bites itself

general to fail on!

Nonetheless, Rah understood that the water was traversable, and there was no danger of animal attacks inform of crocodiles and hippos at this side of the river. He was curious on why Nazaar's army seemed coy on standing immediately on the other side of the river. Were they expecting a slaughter of some sought in the water or a plague of some sought he wondered!

He ordered his army to stand in a straight line horizontally along the river base, and this was very frustrating for Nazaar's army as they saw a vivid and clear picture how large and mighty Rah's army looked across the river bed. However this was what Sierra the Egyptian had anticipated and the poisoned porcupine spikes had been spread throughout the river for this cause.

"*Abafe*[36]!" Rah ordered his army and Tirza commanded the march forward. It was common Bhanda war practice that the strongest factions march behind and the weak are the first inline. Rah had adopted this strategy to try and assess his enemy's war plan but again this was anticipated. Tahia ordered his people to throw *ubudoriro benkukhu*[37]" on the flank that Rah's army was approaching to crossover, and Rah was enraged bythe act.

It was a sign of disrespect which was intolerable too him and his prestige, therefore he told Tirza to instruct every flank and faction to run deep, hard and fast upon their foes and show them no mercy!

"*Abadliwe*[38]" Tirza commanded and the army knew that this meant pure savagery and no mercy indeed. They hit the water running, in-

36 They should die!

37 Chicken's droppings

38 Devour them

fused and infuriated and ready to paint the whole earth red with the blood of their enemies. This was playing exactly according to Sierra's plan, he knew that an infuriated leader was not a thinking strategist and this made Rah vulnerable in his war tactics.

In tens, twenties and hundreds they jumped into the water with focus and sheer will to kill anything on sight, as their general had commanded! One by one the river gods took them as hard and fast as they came. Some of them were not even killed by the spikes but by panic and being tramped as they saw their brothers being claimed by unseen objects in the water. The river was full of blood and a chorus of lamentations from Rah's soldiers and joy from Nazaar's camp. Those that made it across were met with thousands of well sharpened assegais, machetes, spears, axes and various weapons.

It was a fast kill and wait then repeat for Nazaar's people and they were beginning to love it. Rah, on the other side ordered his army to stop and pull-up the corpses! They assembled them in a wide straight line on top of the spike such that they were able to pass unharmed and this marked a turn in events. Rah's army was conditioned for long and large hours of war but most importantly to kill swiftly and fast. This was now personal because they had for the first time lost brothers to a mediocre army, which hadn't even lost any members yet. They therefore killed for more than a necessity and instruction now was, they killed for revenge!

One by one and in thousands Nazaar's army was dismantled. There was nowhere to flee to but only uphill therefore all of Nazaar's army fled accordingly. This made Rah gloat and boast because he knew that his enemies had just sealed their fate for there was no way back and they had trapped themselves near the gorge. What Rah didn't know was playing directly to Sierra's trap.

As many fell and thesoundwaves, of lifeless bodies kept landing on the ground one after the other, a few of Nazaar's people were left, as compared to the ever victorious army of general Rah. Sierra seeing that it was time for the final act of the plan, ordered some of Nazaar's people to roll over the big boulders behind Rah's army, from the mid-point of the mountain and they did this with haste. The sound of the rocks falling and hitting the water made everyone to stop fighting in shock and fear for the first time during the battle.

Nazaar himself was skeptical even though this was his plan together with Sierra. The theory part of the plan was way different and less scary unlike the practical part. There was no need to explain to anyone what had just happened. Rah knew very well that he had been out witted, because whilst he plotted battle strategizes and preservation of his army and resources, his enemy was willing to go beyond the common bylaws of war and die with him and everyone since they were all trapped inside the gorge. This was a well mastered suicide plan and as the water level rose from the big splashes made by the boulders, there was only one way out of this and it was a long jump of death through the waterfall.

As the trapped soldiers wailed trying to swim and get a proper footing in the rising water, Nazaar's army, was bungee jumping for the water fall in 10s and 20s. Rah on the other hand ordered his army to stand close to the large rocks behind them despite the rising water levels. To him, Nazaar and his people were insane and curses from the evil gods that hated the Bhanda kingdom. How could people be just willing to embrace death like that? He pondered.

A warrior's death was surely better that foolish suicide he contemplated but this was a situation that needed an urgent response more than anything else because soldiers were dying in large numbers from drowning and he stampede stomping in the water. The battle of men was surely over, this was a supernatural war now and no one could fight against that with iron and skill. Rah's plan was to let Nazaar and his people jump and kill themselves whislt he and his army would pray to the river and battle gods to save them as they had won the war flawlessly as usual.

Success would surely appease the gods and this would in turn gain them their favor and save them from such an unheroic death but there was something awkward and odd about all the situation. Rah noticed that Nazaar and his 'freak' queen were the first to jump including two uncommon skinned people and a few other Bhanda deserters he knew. At first he thought it was cowardly and in a way Nazaar had robbed him of a death that he had to take from him. However, no one was screaming when they jumped neither did they panic nor even pray for safe passage in the afterlife, as was the custom of warriors as they embraced their death.

When Rah finally saw what was happening, and that there were ropes along the mouth of the waterfall, only 10 of his soldiers were alive including Tirza. Nazaar had instructed the last of his people to use the sharp stones to cut the ropes so that the enemy would be left to meet its fate with no way to escape or chase after them. This was done as commanded by the rightful king of the Bhanda king but two ropes could not be cut fast as intended since most people had lost their sharp knives and machetes in the battle and in the gorge.

These ropes were thicker hence they needed more time, time they didn't have so they left in haste form the caves to the tunnels that connected the mountain. They went to the other side of the plateau where there was dry and clear ground. For Rah and his 10 soldiers, there was only one way! Just an inch of a wave was enough to push all of them over the cliff from the high top of the rocks that they were standing from.

They had survived this long because of rank, which enabled them to be carried to a higher position on the rock side from the rising water levels, as the common soldiers were left to die a common death. Now it was their turn to meet the same fate but no one wanted to die first. These were men that saw Rah as a father and a knight in shining armour, a man to be feared even by the gods but faced with such a calamity, they feared a common and nameless death. You see, even in death, a warrior's name breathes and lives on if he died an honourable death but a common death decays and washes away the legacy therefore no one wanted this.

Rah and his generals had seen the two ropes but it required someone who was a quick swimmer, and extremely lucky! The last of the rocks that were falling from the mountain top, were moving slowly, due to the instability and vibrations that had tilted it as the other rocks fell down and hit it. It was the biggest of the boulders and surely this would doom them all to an immediate death. Since everyone wanted to survive, they all ran into the water and swam towards the ropes in panic and quest to survive.

There was by now, no remembrance of protocols or ranks to be observed, only the will of a man who wanted to survive. This was the only law left, so Rah and his men began to fight in the water for the two ropes. Rah knew that he only had to kill anyone who touched the rope he was close to, and jump immediately, because there was no time for full on combat with and so did Tirza. As the other men were getting deep into the fighting, Rah had managed to kill one of them and grab hold of the rope which he clung onto as fast as he could and jumped over with.

Tirza shortly followed and as he did, the big boulder rolled over in full force and squashed everything in the gorge including Rah's men who were still fighting. The vibrations from the impact the rock made could be felt from every corner of the place, and Rah and Tirza luckily had also made it safely onto the other side of the plateau. They watched as the big boulder made mincemeat out of their brothers and painted the land red with their blood.

It was a deep loss for both sides because in Nazaar's camp, only 300 people survived and all the children had unfortunately died. So it was that the legend of the 300 was born as movies nowadays proclaim in various versions and forms but these were the true sons and daughters of "*Sparta.*" At least the African version of them! Everyone was left wounded spiritually and physically by this war and event that king Nazaar called it "*Inhlungu Ezingapheli*[39]."

As Nazaar and Queen Tahia stood from the other side of the plateau with their subordinates, there saw two men running and following after them. It was clear that their steps were difficult, as there was vibration all over the place from the rocks falling. It was the general himself and Tirzah their enemies! They were the reason why a lot of people had lost their lives and they both looked injured and in urgent need of assistance.

Out of anger and revenge, Queen Tahia ordered her warriors to capture them and behead them. She prophesied to make a canine necklace out of all their teeth, as remembrance of the friends and family she lost because of them. The king understood what was needed and quickly commanded everyone to stand down and assist the two men. There was no medicine or herbs nearby, since the place had been re-

39 The pain that never ends

cently affected by an earthquake and the ground was largely rocky.

As if the gods were with these two men, there was miraculously cabbage that had somehow survived from all the previous hazards up to date. Cabbage can relieve joint pain, arthritis, inflammation and swelling if wrapped all over the body properly and these people knew very well that art.

As Nazaar's people tended to their injured enemies who had been relying on adrenaline all along, the king had a large task and decision up ahead. These men surely had to die eventually for what they had done but they were family as well despite their sudden current state of affairs. These men were heroes of the Bhanda kingdom who had made a name for themselves and deservingly so! If he prolonged their death, his people would begin to lose faith in him and think that he had gone soft.

He feared that his queen would also rally behind them despite their love and this was very dangerous. He could prolong their death long enough to reach the kingdom, in order to make a public example of them to everyone in the Bhanda Empire. Sierra knew very well what he was thinking therefore he gave him a riddle to answer his situation.

Sierra: In Egypt, the blood rendered to the Nile flows opposite to the water but because we drink the water and presume to filter the blood, the river gives life as much as it takes it for the blood of the innocent still laments over the guilty that still survive. Therefore we pour salt into the Nile to dilute the bitterness with the promises of better days and swift judgment! If the body swerves, the mind follows but if the spirit is steadfast and focused then the decision is already made for the

63

world is unfair and decisions sometimes demand sacrifice!

Nazaar understood what this riddle meant and Sierra was right, Tirza and Rah had to die as fast as possible, if he wanted to maintain order in his camp but how was he going to send them to their death he pondered. He could always behead them and keep their heads as trophies to show his treacherous brother when he got home. Or he could give these men the honor and noble act of letting them die in arms, a true hero's death and besides this would give his people some sport to watch and lessons to learn.

For weeks King Nazaar and his people walked through the desert like plateau conquering small tribal groups like the Xhaxha and Moyo tribes, who were known to never shave and bathed with milk instead of water. This was because milk was pure and sanctified for them. General Rah and Tirzah had healed completely but they were prisoners in Nazaar's camp, waiting for their ultimate fate and judgment. They both knew that Nazaar was going to kill them but they didn't know how he was going to do it.

For weeks, Nazaar had dodged talking to them but weirdly instructed his subordinates to treat them like royalty and to never dare poison their food as some would want to do. As Nazaar kept conquering on his way back home, to reclaim the throne as the rightful heir, his army kept on expanding and getting stronger. The 300 was always distinguished from the other people as they were personally trained by both Nazaar himself and Queen Tahia. They had nothing to lose anymore and they fought likewise.

Every kill was like an addiction for them, they couldn't get enough of the sight of spilling their enemies' bowels and blood all over the place.

64

Even Rah was impressed of how the 300 had mastered the art of war, he felt proud of Nazaar in a way.

Emalahleni

In all his conquests, Nazaar had cleverly made show that he was always clear of the vicinity and whereabouts of the Egyptians and borderlines of Bhanda territory. This was because he knew that if he was too quick to go back home, Theodore would kill him and his people before they even made it to the capital, therefore he needed an army of his own. Above all, he needed a spectacle that would sway every Bhanda tribe's support and allegiance to him as the rightful king.

This is why he had refused to kill the general and Tirza because they were crucial for this plan to work. His subordinates had questioned his decision but because they feared him, they had no choice but to respect what he had done for them so far. They believed he had a plan that would eventually end with the demise of their nemeses. Queen Tahia wanted to kill them herself but when Nazaar had told her of his plan, she agreed completely with her husband.

The plan was easy, Theodore would rally out every warrior of the Bhanda kingdom when he had heard that Nazaar and his army were coming. As the might of all the Bhanda Empire rallied behind their self-made king to war. Every chief would be available to deputize the king and be in charge of their various tribes. Most chiefs hated Theodore and Rah for their dictatorship and how they had assumed power and treated them. Theodore had absurdly ruled like his father and because he evoked fear from his subordinates, this meant that there was extreme punishment for anyone that didn't bend to his will, or pay his high tribute demands in time.

Nazaar knew all of this very well for he had sent his scouts and spies for some days, to gather information on the current state of affairs in the Bhanda kingdom, and all of them reported similar news. Before parties engaged in war, the two kings and a number of their emissaries had to meet in a sacred and mutually consented ground to talk, and possibly test the enemy's determination to continue with the war. No lives would lost during this meeting and all weapons were to be left outside the sacred grounds.

This was Nazaar's grand opportunity to appeal and appease the Bhanda chiefs to ally with him, as he would give them one of the things that they never thought that they would see in their lifetime. A bonfire was going to be ablaze, its breadth covering ten metres whilst the length covered yet another ten metres.

This would be called the ring of fire that Tirza and general Rah were to meet their fate. Both men were going to fight bare footed, on the burning charcoal, with no armour and definitely with no weapons. It was a savage fight to death but it was an advantage to the loser to die that way but for the winner, he was going to suffer even more. The winners' life wasn't his anymore even in victory, it belonged to the kingdom and the king therefore he could choose what to do with it as he pleased.

Finally after some days of battle preparations in both camps, the time came for the two kings and brothers to meet in the sacred ground. Theodore dreaded to meet his big brother, because deep down he knew that he had betrayed him deeply, and there was no turning back to what he had done. Nazaar on the other hand wanted nothing more than killing Theodore, and everyone who had assisted him in the *coup de tat* and his father's murder.

He wanted to pluck out his brother's heart whilst it was still beating, and devour it before him as he lost all consciousness in death. This was just one of the revenge strategies he always thought about, in a pool of countless ways of decapitating his treacherous brother. When the two factions arrived at the sacred ground, Theodore surprised everyone by running towards his brother and hugging him tight as they spoke privately for a while in their brotherly embrace.

King Theodore: Even after all, the gods still rally in your favour brother! (*grinning*)

King Nazaar: Even after your treachery, you still soundlike the young boy I was sending to gather firewood for me dear king! (*grinning*)

King Theodore: We are sons of a great man aren't we brother?

King Nazaar: Indeed we are even if you killed him!

King Theodore: It was fate that he had to fall big brother. Remember, if the moon is touched by the darkness then the night is longer and danger to the prey is certain but if light prevails then better days lie ahead.

King Nazaar: Even the moon seeks permission from the day to shine and light at night, because it is nature and was deemed by the gods but it fades away into the dark because like every emissary of greatness, you have to give others a chance to be born and live to the legend of those who chose to shine before times, real kings, true royalty, not thievery of power and abomination of spilling your own blood!

King Theodore: So you seek to do this abomination as well? Spilling your own blood, your brothers' blood?

King Nazaar: I am the ancestors and the gods' hand of vengeance upon everyone who took part in killing my father, for even if he made mistakes, it didn't change that he was king and my father. I am my Father's reckoning against all the guilty and I made my peace a long time ago when I buried all our relatives that you sent your clowns to kill including me, you remember?

As was custom of the wrong to the wronged, Theodore at that moment, saw the full map and scope of the pain he had caused and done, and it broke him into pieces internally but there was no going back. The only thing that was left was to proceed with the *inyembezi zokucina* cultural procedure before either one of them died. Each brother had to cry until they could no more shed a tear. The last tear was to be collected by hand by the other brother, and they would take a pinch of soil from the ground and rub their hands together with the tears.

This was a sign that their bond had been cut off, and even their ancestors were to accept it but most importantly, it signified that the winner would not mourn for the dead brother, for they had already done it for them when they were alive. To those who watched the spectacle, it was sad because this indeed was the division of brotherhood. Not only that but a nation, friendships, family bonds and ties, because after that ceremony there was no going back.

If one's relative was on the enemy's rank or army, they had to face a merciless death, as it was law and culture to follow ones chosen king to the death if it demanded. This was the last civil and sentimental act of peace, respect and love for everyone who was there, thus when the two brothers were weeping, all, from the chiefs to the best warriors had to bow down and put their hands forward in a prayer position. This was done facing towards their enemies as a sign of honouring the presence of the two kings and the royals in both armies. They had to stay in this position to the end. Shedding tears with the kings was a taboo, therefore to avoid this, both camps would sing universal Bhanda songs to avoid any emotional attachment to the scenario.

After a while, everything was complete, the parties knew that the brothers knew that war had begun.

King Theodore: Don't hold back brother for I am no longer the little brother you used to know and I promise to give you the best fight of your life and look you straight in the eyes when I take your life.

King Nazaar: Let it be known that I have become death! The eater of worlds and destroyer of lives for brother, the emptiness and darkness of our condemned fallen brethren awaits you *esihogweni*[40], I am the tip, the very thrust of pain that will pierce and behead you! My children and I will drink from the skulls of your children, who shall be royal slaves for eternity to my house. Every boy child in your

40   In eternal fire

lineage shall be cast *ebhalwini lwabo malulwane*[41] and the cave will decide his fact! I am the undisputed champion of Bhanda, first of my nature, last of my kind and you dare challenge my birth right and resent me! "*Ma intando yamakhosi yenziwe.*[42]

King Thedore: Ma intando yamakhosi yenziwe!

Soon after the two former brothers had spoken and said their peace, it was time for the main event of the day and king Nazaar's surprise. Bound and in bad shape, Rah and Tirza were dragged and bound by *imisila kakondo*[43]. Every member of King Theodore's camp especially the king himself, were shocked. No one had ever thought, or even dreamt that strong and well accomplished men such as Rah and Tirza could fall to such a level.

Well, here they were, a laughing stock too many chiefs they had bullied into tribute, under the authority of a king they didn't love and believe in! Theodore was lost for words, this was the worst possible start to a war, ever! If his warriors had the slightest fear for Nazaar before, they would surely break a sweat at the sight of him now! The great Rah, the greatest schemer, shrewd arm and chaperon of the king, the "iron chancellor of Africa" for the history fanatics, had finally fallen from grace! In shekels, frail and a little malnourished, the former gen-

41   A bat cave were a mysterious creature was deemed to reside and feed of anything that intruded or visited the cave
42   Let the will of the gods be done
43   Squirrel tails tied together

eral looked weaker than he had ever been.

The war for him was now an eternal one as he had literally became an addict and insane due to the large quantities of *ntsangu*[44] that Tahia had secrectly ordered the slave caterers to put in both Tirza and Rah's meals and *umqombothi*[45] when they would drink. As it was custom for the Bhanda men whether free or slaves to drink from Friday to Sunday, so did they. These were days rendered to the harvest gods as the Bhanda kingdom was also largely an agricultural empire, hence drinking excessively and taking excessive marijuana was deemed as spiritual, and intimate meditation that brought someone closer to the ancestors. In Rah and Tirza's case it had become daily bread, due to Tahia's servants, spiking their food and liquor.

This wasn't poison as king Nazaar had warned against but it surely was also a slow death that Tahia knew very well would work if done correctly and patiently. As Nazaar ordered his servants to free the two slaves, all sat down except for him and Theodore. Rah and Tirzah were dragged near the ring of fire which was ready to burn and roast the guilt out of them all literally!

| King Nazaar: | These are your champions, the proud jewels of the Bhanda kingdom, men of war, and our brothers and to some our fathers! I weep deeply for these men today because even if indlulamithi sent our finest to kill me, the gods blessed me and gave me favour from my adversaries! Jabbari, Yemen, Ulah, Fazak, Mirriam, Barzukar, Sheilah, Ruth, Ndoda, |

44 Marijuana

45 African beer

Mfalakhe, Mbuyazwe, Thenjiwe, Khalaza, Nandi, Mondli, Velile and Vuyisile, these are the names of first blood royals, sons and daughters of royalty that these men murdered, as they tried to get to me and I buried my family in sorrow.. The law condemns anyone who murders a royal family member without fair grounds of war and a sealed treaty witnessed and approved by the gods. Rah and Tirzah acted under the order of *iguqa leli*[46]! Unfortunately today we are here to witness their judgment as it is custom in our lands that treason and cowards are dealt with by fire and smoke. My chiefs, my people and every Bhandanian witnessing this today, hear me! I am your true King and because some of you have questioned my birth right by their action, witness therefore my mercy and judgement as the gods have guided me to punish my enemies. *Ntshonalanga, Nyakatho Ningizimu, Mpumalanga,*[47] *badleni, Makhosi amadala!*[48]

Ntshonalanga, Ningizimu, Mpumalanga, Nyakatho were believed to be great gods who moved the sun, moon, day and night at their will. There was no compass, no direction, people prayed to these gods for wind, sunlight

46   This calf
47   West, South, East and North
48   Kill them, great gods

and even rainfall sometimes, as they believed each piece of life was placed specifically for a time and purpose that only these gods could reveal to those that believed in the shapeless, and directionless world. These were the 4 chief gods that sat at the realm of the Bhanda spiritual realm and only kings were allowed to talk to them or about them!

As King Theodore stood there, shocked and contemplating his nextmove, Rah and Tirzah were escorted inside the ring of fire, as they grimaced in pain and heat emanating from the hot charcoal. A true warrior went out in style and faced his destiny without fear. That was a custom in the Bhanda kingdom! This meant that showing emotion in war was a sign of weakness, and for these two man, there was no room for even an inch of excuse because they were legends.

These two were some of the greatest warriors ever to be produced by the kingdom despite the unfortunate future they faced. There was no time for pleasantries and unnecessary last words, these men despite their physical and mental condition at the time, were still formidable machines of war. In a matter of seconds, charcoal was flying all over as these men engaged in a ruthless brawl. They strangled, twisted and turned for unseen advantages as the smoke was clouding the place.

The game plan was mutual on both ends, kill your opponent as fast as possible and minimize the burns and the probability of being scorched! Both camps chose 10 warriors each and these men stood as the rings' ropes and boundary. One of their task was to make sure that the ring of fire maintained its ruthless heat. Thus that meant that they poured pig oil onto the charcoal periodically, to keep the charcoal alight, red and burning! After some minutes of fighting with gusto, these men found themselves in a stalemate.

This wasn't because both of them were equally good but it was because Rah was holding up and buying himself time for "the final move. Rah and Tirzah had also out maneuvered Tahia's plan. They knew very well that someone would eventually try to assassinate or poison them therefore they took *isizilo* to always take every meal and liquid substance with charcoal water norder to counter any toxic or harmful substance that might be poured into their food and drinks.

Everyone had to think that they had gone insane if they stood, a chance to survive the amount of days that they did. Therefore they did the best they did to imitate being crazy and everyone actually bought it because they did a splendid job. The former general's plan was easy, prolong the fight until both kings bit their finger nails and threw them to the ground. This was an act of soiling the battlefield after two enemies were at par and the fight had gone too long.

The fighting had to be taken to another intense level where the two warriors were to be given weapons. Their feet had to be tied up such that the participants would only pivot with their legs but completely rely on their hands, wits and weapons to win. It was a draw and kill fight, a cowboy standout classic gunfight for the readers that obsess about raw action.

However this was sacred ground which forbade the usage of typical war weapons such as assegai's, bow and arrows and swords therefore the two warriors had to partake in a*Rungu*"fight and throwing spectacle.

A rungu is a wooden throwing club or baton bearing special symbolism and significance. It was largely associated with morans (male warriors) who traditionally used it in warfare and for hunting. Rungus were typically about 45–50 cm (18–20 inches) in length with a long narrow shaft for a handle and heavy knob or ball at the end in the manner of other indigenous cudgels such as the Irish shillelagh or South African knobkierie.

74

In the Bhanda culture, the *rungu* was an important emblem of warrior status for males. A special one was held by the king at important tribal gatherings. Both Theodore and Nazaar held them at important public gatherings. King Theodore held an elegant gold or silver-tipped ivory *rungu*. He referred to it as *induku yamabala* and would pound it on the "table of law when angry, sometimes shattering the skulls of those condemned to death with it in order to speed up the many cases he had to attend and judge as King, and the jury and sovereign law.

King Nazaar correspondingly to his nick name as *uMnyamana*[49] held a black *rungu* that had been carved out of the hip bone of *uMahambayedwa*[50] that he had killed. This was a tale that had actually sealed his fate as the undisputable champion of the Bhanda kingdom because every warrior that had went to the great mountain of Nyanga had never came back. If they did, it was only their emblem that made back home as the wind and gradient would blow and push it back to the capital. To further announce another win to the great ape and lose to the great kingdom!

When Nazaar came back from the mountain holding its head, even his father, the late king Menelick understood that he was standing in the presence of a great man. No one knew why the bones of the defeated ape were black but the assumption was that it was because it was an ancient evil that had stood the test of time.

Since the *rungu* fight was also a form of cultural bet and game to entertain people especially the royals, it was custom for the two kings to avail their *rungu's*, to the champions that were to represent them in

49   The dark one

50   The biggest ape known as King Kong to some today

the duet.

Defeat was not an exception as it would be embarrassing to the king who lost. This was however a different case, since both men were from the same camp. This meant that they had to use the local medical doctors' *rungu's* which were used to panel beat dislocated bones. It took one strike to kill a man with a *rungu* if a skilled expert held it. Rah and Tirzah knew very well that the fight was nearing its end as they were both given *rungu's*.

Rah: You have fought well and served your kingdom my son!

Tirzah: I learnt from the best father but I know that I have to embrace my fate now, as we all know that you will surely defeat me eventually. We can prolong this as long as we desire but we are burning for a cause that no longer has meaning. I bled for this kingdom, for both these kings, my brothers but look at me today, I fight for their amusement, their mercy, for their favour! This is not how we the Bhanda do things. We are proud men, men of war but most importantly men of honour and respect! I ask one last favour father! Hit hard and hit straight and may the gods that saved you before, come to your rescue again but remember to fulfil the prophecy we dreamt of during the full moon.

Rah: *Hamba kahle ndodana[51].*

The great general said these words crying and screaming in agony as he hit Tirzah hard on the forehead, killing him instantly. Tirzah didn't even try to block, he had accepted his fate and he knew that Rah was the man needed to accomplish the prophecy that even the late king Menelick had spoken about. As Tirzah fell, no one screamed for joy or congratulated Rah for the win. Both kings had lost a brother and someone they saw and treated as family from when they were young. It was a very sad day for both camps but it also sparked a full on war.

To further humiliate Thedore, king Nazaar ordered his servants to pluck out Rah's eyes and queen Tahia did not waste any time in assuming the chance to revenge against her enemy. She quickly plucked them out as her servants held Rah. Nazaar took the eyes and threw them in the ring of fire were Tirzah's corpse was slowly catching fire and burnt to dust.

Rah never cried or begged for mercy, but he begged Nazaar to throw him into the Ngalade river were the biggest and fiercest of the crocodiles lived. Everyone was shocked by this but then again, Rah wasn't any normal Bhanda man, this was a champion, a man who had never known defeat. Most importantly, he was the man who embraced the will of the gods.

Nazaar granted him his wish and ordered Tahia to see to it that she brings back Rah's emblem as a token and trophy. This was also a way of remembering him when the crocodiles had dismembered his body, because indeed he was a true Bhanda and a legend despite everything else.

Due to the Bhanda custom, the winner takes and says all. Theo-

---

51   Go well son

dore had been indirectly beaten on the first battle, even though it wasn't a direct war. This showcase of power by Nazaar had actually weakened him in front of his chiefs but it also evoked a level of evil, revenge and rage that he had never felt before. He knew he couldn't fight his brother there due towar rules and customs but he swore to make his brothers world quake from that day on. Nazaar on the other hand understood that the first phase of returning and claiming his throne had been done, know came the tougher part, war!

This was going to be a long war and the threat from Egypt and other rising kingdoms didn't make it any easy. If an opportunistic kingdom came whilst they were spilt and in a civil war like this, it could spell disaster for the empire, as they would be vulnerable to invasion. Sadly, this was the only way and so both camps went their separate ways earmarking the place as *ukuqhaqheka kwenkaba.*[52]

The battle was set to begin after 2 days when the moon had settled. As for Rah, Queen Tahia and her servants threw him in the *Ngalade* River, as he had asked but the waves just carried him away from their sight. The assumption was that he was definitely going to die, because either the water would drown him as he was now blind, or the crocodiles would totally dismember him. However Rah's fate was far from over!

---

52 Separation of the belly button, meaning the separation of the family

Chapter Three

Family

As the Bhanda empire was bracing itself for a local brawl to death, time and years had passed and the illegitimate son of the former king Menelick had grown, stronger, wiser and more complex. No one knew what he was or even dared to believe that he was human. Everyone assumed he was one of Glenda's evil things therefore he was called the *ingane yomthakathi*[53]. Kane never cared nor paid attention to any of it. He knew he was different from the moment he learnt to speak. Looking at himself and those who surrounded him, he was an obvious mismatch.

If he was to matter in this world which had already classified him as a thing and a worthless outcast, he had to go above and beyond to earn that respect, and Glenda also knew that very well. Although everyone was an outcast in Glenda's community, no one wanted to play with the albino because he was viewed as the worst of the curse to ever fall on the earth. Faced with a reality of segregation, Kane embraced the dark.

He only shared his love and light for Glenda, the only friend, mother and person who ever mattered and treated him like a human being. Glenda imparted him with as much wisdom as she had on enchantments, and day to day livelihood but most importantly, to hate her nemeses, the royals! The outcasts were customarily called by the

53   Son of the witch

king when there was war for one purpose only. If an outcast wanted to earn the right to be recognized as a Bhandananian once again, he or she had to be willing be a sacrifice for the empire for the greater cause of the elite.

This usually meant being at the fore front! This is where people generally died before they even got the chance to throw a spear or unsheathe their swords and axes, because of the intensity and the initial contact of the armies. This was a tactic to save the real Bhanda warriors as much as possible, and at the same time to exhaust the enemy. If an outcast survived that or if the outcast army won the battle before the real army stepped in, then it was deemed as a blessing from the gods. This would make them to be recognized as Bhanda people again.

If they died, or were obliterated by the enemy, it was viewed as good riddance and the right punishment from the gods. Arrows, spears and dust were all over the place as the two kings clashed for the ultimate right to the Bhanda throne. Kane had never been to war but he was a resourceful young man when it came to fighting. In his community, teenagers his age used to bully him but most of them used to find themselves on the ground before they could even finish making fun of him.

He used to train alone by hitting bamboo trees until they would fall and crack to his bloody knuckles. That was when he was just 10years old and by the time he was a teenager, he had cleared out most of the bamboos for farming. This he achieved through kicking them down. He was a strong man and even worse, a child born different, full of anger and a thirst for revenge and evil.

Back at the battlefield, months had passed and war was still on. None of the former brothers looked to be virtually winning because they used the same battle tactics and art of war. The amount of dead bodies was the only alarming reality. Bhanda soldiers were dying in their thousands for a cause that could have been avoided, if the brothers had just fought between themselves and saved everyone else their lives and time. Nonetheless, it was custom and law that the brothers could only fight amongst themselves, if there was a direct and foreign threat to the empire as this would fast-track and determine who the people would rally behind for such a sudden eventuality.

The Ngulade River was the middle point between the two kings as it divided the two areas that they ruled in the meantime. King Theodore ruled the entire Bhanda Empire with the same territories that his father used to rule over. King Nazaar on the other hand ruled all the outlands as he had conquered many tribes in his quest for power. Since the people who lived near and along the Ngulade River were largely outcasts, both kings felt like they could use them as bait in war.

Nazaar liked the idea that most of them were known witches and wizards but most importantly, he knew that they hated his young brother more because of the l"law of the forgotten". This was a law that Theodore had passed in his first term as king. Under this law, everyone cursed or cast away by the king was deemed to inherit that fate even up to the afterlife. No favour was to be given to that person, they were to be simply, forgotten! This meant that every outcast had one chance at gaining the gods and king's favour and that was through being vessels of war.

Mpuku inge watwela mu bwina bwa mfuko kuvulanyako.
"If a mouse enters into the hole of a mole, forget about it." This was a primordial saying derived from the tale of an ancient place that had the most unique slope in the world. When someone was standing on highland, the area looked like it had a caldera/crater or a hole on the ground such as the present day Bermuda triangle. When someone

81

was on low ground on the surface, the land seemed to be upside down, and the stars always seemed to be at a touching distance. The place was filled with unlimited and complex realities and hallucinations. This was a place that gave the dreams it took and took the people it gave them to.

No one survived this place because it was an ancient enchantment that pre-dates even the dawn of the immaculate *inkakha/ kgaga/ haka/ khwara*[54]. 100 masters of the dark arts had sacrificed their lives in that place, as a means of advocating for mercy, for fellow generations of wizards and witches to come. It was however deemed that the gods refused to grant them favour, therefore their spirits lurked around the area, wandering about, and trapping everyone in the spiritual world of endless hallucinations and dreams.

This meant that that an hour spent on the spiritual cloud around the area would be about ten days in reality. Hence, most people died before they could even finish their dreams or accomplish their quests in the physical world. It was the darkest of ancient traps and enchantments and it could not be broken.

Today, *mpuku inge watwela mu bwina bwa mfuko kuvulanyako* is an African Swahili proverb meaning *"you don't expect to win a case in someone else's village or place,"* and indeed this was true of the following events that transpired. You see both kings now wanted to lay claim over the outcasts and their lands, therefore a war for the Ngulade area was imminent. This was the final war that was to decide who was to rule over the entire Bhanda empire and who was to perish. *Mpuku inge watwela mu bwina bwa mfuko kuvulanyako* was a myth to outsiders but a defence mechanism for the Ngulade dwellers.

In true honesty and bareness, it was just an area full of fog and

54 Pangolin.

the apparent mystery surrounding the existence of the dark hole from an eagle's eye view which was just a dry valley, full of ambitious and countless skeletons at the bottom. The real enchantment wasn't the spell that was cast on the place but it was on the hype and general norm that those that went around the place never came back. It was said they would be blind sighted by the deep layer of fog, hence falling into the valley without seeing were there were going.

So the stage was set! If the two kings wanted the Ngulade, they had to fight over it but that was if they could manage to survive it first because this was the land of outcasts, the land of pure evil.

The Ngulade War (The Nightmare War/ *Impi Yamaphupho amabi*)

Mathematics was incubated in Africa. Ancient African tribes such as the Bhanda and *Anu* people used maths, not only to build and to tell time which helped with crops but also to structure war and map out best and possible areas of advantage, attack and defence. Nazaar already had a team of 5 captive and wise Egyptians that he trusted under the command of their leader Sierra. Egyptians were unrivalled in mathematics and strategy that is, they could mathematically study anything with accurate symmetry and conviction.

Theodore also had masters of the art and a weapon of his own, Tasmanians or the Palawa people! The Palawa people were known for their curled hair which was often tight and skin colours that ranged from black to reddish-brown. One of their most prominent features was their broad noses, wide mouths, and sets of deep brown eyes, which gave them an ancient and medieval look and the nick name, *Black Aborigines*.

They were not pygmies but they were short, and some of them could easily be passed for pygmies, with their little body fat, which made them *plump*. Theodore had invaded their lands and enslaved them because he didn't consider the Palawa to be humans, although he acknowledged that they were naturally wise and peaceful.

The exploitation of the Tasmanian people by the Bhanda people under Theodore was very sadistic, and barbaric. They only saw them as weapons and equipment of wisdom and mathematics and nothing more. They had served the Bhanda Empire in some of their conquests and Theodore was a fan of their work. In reality, they were one of the cleverest tribes that could probably challenge the Egyptian might in mathematics and strategy.

On a different note, Rah had miraculously survived the jaws of the crocodiles in the Ngulade River, and drowning, as the water had pushed him up to the river bank. This was a small branching stream from the *Ngulade* River called *ezinatha khona*.[55] This was the place where most outcasts took their livestock to drink because it was safe from the crocodiles. Since the waters were shallow, this meant most people, especially herdsmen would frequent the place.

As Rah's seemingly lifeless body was floating on the water, approaching the drinking place, only the albino was around the drinking zone. He saw a man's being carried by the mighty waters and Kane was quick to fish him out with *ingwegwe*.[56] Initially, Kane thought that Rah was just another blind outcast that wanted to commit suicide and had thrown himself in the river, hoping that the crocodile or the water would kill him but unfortunately he had survived.

55   Where they drink
56   A wooden hook-like long stick

Punishment for someone who had tried to commit suicide and the medication to wake up someone who had passed out was the same, wasps and bees! Whoever saved such a person had to find 5 wasps and 5 bees and put them on the person's back The insects would naturally sting the person to cautiousness but the pain that was left after the stings, had been removed and the swelling was deemed to be his/her punishment, and a reminder that the gods still had a purpose for them on earth.

So young Kane did as the law demanded and Rah woke up almost jumping at the rapid and painful stinging. If he still could see he would have broken Kane's jaw or killed him in anger for what he had done but he was now just a shadow of his former self. After Rah had cooled down, Kane asked him who he was and why he had committed the coward's act of suicide but Rah wasn't interested in talking with the young boy. Rah had one mission and that mission had to be executed very swiftly therefore he answered the young man with a question of his own.

Rah: Does it matter who I am and what I did young man? You are young and boys your age are at the regiments of the king, why are you here herding livestock instead of fighting and growing with other warriors?

Kane: What is a warrior old man? A slave or a weapon of the elite who wipe their sweat with the efforts and blood of those that condemn themselves to a futile death? All for the misguided misconception of legacies and heroism! I don't have a king because I am my own king and in this jungle I roam and rule alone. You are very lucky that you are blind old man, because if you could see who you were talking to then you would understand! Seems like they removed your eyes with a burning sharp object, what were you before and what did you do to deserve such cruelty?

Rah: I envy you young man, I can tell that you are a very clever young lad and your parents must be very proud of you. Everyone needs a king, a leader and a father to show them the way, direction and ultimately link them to the gods. You see my boy, kings are not just mere man, they are chosen before times by a peculiar consortium of elect and-divine powers that make them physical and spiritual descendants of the gods, and our anchor to the afterlife! Such is the reality of life young man but enough of these time wasting pleasantries! Do you know an old witch by the name of Glenda the Horrible? It is of paramount and pressing essence that I meet the woman because the fate of our people depends on it!

Kane: I do not know her but I can assist you to locate her, I am sure it won't be hard to find a "horrible witch" as you say!

Rah: Lead the way young blood! And hold me by hand

86

as we go. This blindness is a new feature in my life and I have to conceal my face so that I am not seen because if I am...! We won't even reach where we intend to go to!

This troubled young Kane very much as he began to wonder who this old man was. "What he had done? And why would people want to kill him instantly if ever they saw his face?"

The former General knew very well that the outcasts hated him and Theodore equally, for all they had done to them, and if they had a chance to revenge upon him they wouldn't hesitate. Only the young didn't know fully well who Rah was because time had flown past with unending wars, and foreign expeditions where the former general was before his eventual fate.

From his physique and grip as they strode along to Glenda and Kane's home, young Kane could tell that this was a great warrior once! As they approached Glenda's home, a strong whirlwind circulated around them but Kane knew very well that this was the work of his mother, therefore he only had to command it to stop and it faded away at his command. He didn't want to do that abruptly, he wanted to see how Rah would react to the whirlwind but to his surprise the former general laughed and commanded it to stop himself.

To Kane's amazement it stopped instantly and his home was open and clear for them to see. Before he could even mutter the guile to ask what had just happened, Glenda was behind them! Rah smirked because young Kane was overwhelmed by this until he knelt down not knowing what to do but Rah rebuked him, saying it was a taboo for him to kneel in front of such *evil*.

Glenda the horrible: Hello brother, so you finally arrive!

Rah: Indeed little sister! But before we all accept our fates, please hear me first!

Glenda the horrible: No brother, before you embrace your death, say your last words! Today you come as a destitute at the front gate of my house, looking for mercy? Bloody mercy! Nah Rahzagul Kahut, we are the children of abomination. One must die! One had to die and the axe of death still awaits your blood as the custom states. Did you tell him who and what you are?

Rah: I survived this long to get here because it wasn't my time yet Glendaratsi Kahut! I know I deserve the edge of your sword or the swift death from your powerful and potent magic but you saw the vision and the stars. The boy is in great danger, if both his brothers know that he is alive, everyone will die and they would burn you alive. War is coming to the plains of *Ngulade* very soon and most of these people won't make it! *"Ayabhonsa amathole kaDabuza, isizwe sonakele*[57]*!"* But that is nothing compared to what is coming dear sister. The boy must begin his journey now before it is too late!

57 The two brothers are at war and the empire is divided

Kane: Wait! This man is your twin brother, mother?
                     Why have you never told me about him?

Glenda the horrible: This thing was dead to me son before today! He
                     indeed is my flesh and blood but according to the
                     Kahut tradition we both had to be killed since we
                     were twins, or kill each other when we reached
                     adulthood. That would be a way of thanking
                     the gods for the leniency and life they had given
                     us. This was meant to bless our family more,
                     and guarantee a royal seat for them in the after-
                     life! However our mother did an abomination of
                     running away with us but she was killed and fed
                     in pieces to the vultures. That was done by our
                     father, who wanted to offer us for sacrifice! For-
                     tunately before she died, our mother had hidden
                     us very well and gave us new names and common
                     people's crests to make us blend well and main-
                     tain our cover, as another family of the Gereze
                     tribe adopted us! As we grew, we were separated
                     because we were identical twins and Rah hadn't
                     grown a beard yet, people would have noticed the
                     abomination therefore, Rahzagul was adopted
                     and conscripted into the Bhanda army by the late
                     King Menelick, when he was just a prince whilst I
                     remained with the common people.

Kane: Then why do you hate him so much when it was your family and the stupid gods' fault that separated you mother?

Glenda the horrible: Oh! Pity you don't know my sweet boy! Years passed and this man became the general of the Bhanda kingdom. He never looked for me nor did he care what happened to me. When I was condemned to these lands he was there, laughing with our enemies and he is the one who told them to cut out my big toes as punishment for a crime that I never committed. I was a happy young woman once son, with a handsome husband and a future to look forward too but this man and the royals took it all away from me!

Rah: Who do you think killed Maliq and all the witness who supported his assertion after your judgement? Who do you think begged the king not to kill you but punish you? Maybe it's not love or maybe it's nothing at all but I never forgot you *mntakamama*[58], I simple had to stay away from you in order to protect you! I am sorry for everything that happened to you and all the pain you have suffered. King Menelick was an immoral and cunning man and at the end of the day he had to be put down, or else we would have all perished with him. We managed to stage a coup and assas-

58   Mother's child

sinate him but all of this has come at a huge cost of my dignity and eyesight. I only grieve and plead for communion with the gods as I aim to appease them one last time before I meet my final stand. Look at us! Twins with messed up eyesight and countless scars! (Chuckles)

Glenda the horrible: Well you were always the naughty one that's why they took both of your eyes out and left me with one to see the road! (Giggles)

Rah: You still got dumb jokes little sister! (Grins). Don't worry this time around I will teach you better and no one will ever hurt you again!

Kane: So mother this is my uncle? I am pleased to finally have a male figure especially an accomplished warrior but how will I learn to be as great as you uncle when you have become blind and even worse, I will never be accepted in the Bhanda kingdom no matter what!

Rah: With what is coming my son, it won't matter who loves who and who wants to kill who but only who will survive. There shall come a day when you will be alone and no one will be there to even refresh your body with ointment and oil from the desert heat and fowls of the northern lands! Don't worry about being accepted by your people my son but worry about saving what would be left of them because the days of the great slaughter are nigh! You were born different could tell when I touched your skin but that has made you even more special and strong. Boys your age are still pygmies and dwarfs but like your brothers and fore fathers you are a giant and the blood of great king's flows through you! I may not be able to see any more but I can still hear a man breathing through the pores of his nostrils from 10 paces away and I can pluck out his Adam's ample without him even feeling it! Learn and endue the pain because we no longer have time!

Glenda the horrible: I have taught all I can my son, now it is another's turn and burden to guide the *king*! The men that will come here, are indeed your brothers but they will seek to destroy everything you love and unfortunately they will succeed! I will not make it out of the tide that is coming as I have seen in the vision but the gods will guide you my son!

Kane: I will kill anyone who touches you mother, to hell with prophecy, damn the gods! They shall all feel my wrath and edge of the sword, let them come, let them try. "I grew up alone..."

Glenda the Horrible   ...Die alone!"

Rah: Let the lessons begin!

"Born alone and die alone," were the last words that Rah and Glenda's mother had spoken to them, and they kept these words as an everyday motto. Kane was indoctrinated to this motto of survival of the fittest, as he was also a child born into hardships. He saw Glenda and Rah as parental figures but also as heroes, since they were the only people who actually recognised him as more than just a human being or thing as other people called him. Rah taught him the art of war and everything he knew about hand to hand combat, using practical elements of the earth that surrounded them such as water.

It got so intense on some days that Kane had to run over a sea of charcoal and thorns as punishment for failing just one thing, out of many. Every sandal he had was used to fuel the fire as Rah believed in stealth and efficiency in combat, thus sandals made a warrior slow and slow in a battle meant death. This is something that even Nazaar and Theodore were taught at a very young age. On the 3rd month of Kane's intensive training, Theodore's legions stood on the east of the Ngulade plateau and Nazaar's army stood on the west!

The preparation for the war had took months but it finally came and boy did it come! This was the war that broke and created many kingdoms and varies languages and cultural distinctions in Africa. The first to attack was Nazaar as usual because he never believed in waiting for an enemy to attack first, it was a sign of weakness to him. Theodore was never one to shy away from a good fight, therefore he rallied his troops behind him and led them head first towards their enemies.

Since the brothers had taken the oath of *no tears* for the fallen, it was believed to be was abominable to die screaming or making noise, because it could condemn one to lose acknowledgement, and a place in the afterlife. It was the most savage battle ever recorded, but even more astonishing, the most silent as most of the warriors had bitten of the front parts of their tongues, sawn their lips together or bit some strong card to avoid screaming or making noise at the possibility of a sudden death.

No soldier wanted to die for nothing and the king's word was judgement in the world above and below. Blood was splattered all over the place to a point that the *Ngulade* crocodiles and hippos fled from the frenzy instead of enjoying the free meals that came from the lacerations of metal, bone and flesh. The ground had become slippery to a point that some of the troops were crawling to reach their enemies, being smeared in the blood whilst trying to balance themselves. It was also to avoid falling upon their enemies' blade without even being attacked directly.

For the outcasts of the *Ngulade*, there was no room to escape! For every fallen warrior on the battlefield, they screamed and cried because they understood that it didn't matter who won but their fate would be the same either way! Nazaar wanted to use them as pones in his foreign policy whilst Theodore just wanted to kill them all slowly, to appease the gods to acknowledge him as the greatest king ever and also train his young regiments to kill real moving targets. As the war kept on getting nearer to the villages, some of the outcasts were caught in the cross fire and were killed.

When some mercenaries from Theodore's army were close to Glenda's village, word spread fast that they wanted to kill all abnormal and disabled people. This was because they neither saved the purpose of war and greatness for any side. They were viewed as a waste of time and human genes, therefore they had to be executed as fast as possible. As for the albino, Kane was to be executed instantly if ever he was seen.

One by one, the cries and blood of the fallen disabled outcasts was splattered all over the place. When they reached Glenda's house, the Bhanda soldiers knew very well that Glenda was the most powerful witch in this land, therefore they smeared their bodies with salt and poured around the place. This was a way of protecting themselves against her magic but they didn't know that her greatest trick was just one angry and capable young boy, who had the guidance of one capable and blind warrior!

Just as he used to break the bamboo trees with one punch and kick, Kane wasted no time breaking the bones of his fellow compatriots. Rah on the other hand, was on a crazy spree of his own, beheading everyone he could reach with his double edged swords that Glenda had specifically forged for him due to his blindness.

Theodore's men were too many for just two people to handle therefore, Rah instructed Kane to run to the hills where he was to pass through the trenches of Zipler. From there he was to travel north and never stop until he met a man by the name of Naimer.

Kane took the last sights in of his mother Glenda in stride as Theodore's men slew her and at the same time overpowered Rah and captured him. This wasn't a time cry or stop and Kane understood this. He ran for his life as his enemies followed him in hot pursuit. As fate would have it, Theodore's men met a contingent of Nazaars men, coming from a neighbouring village and the battleline was drawn, allowing Kane to break free and escape quietly. Nazaar's men over powered Theodore's and slew all of them until the captured Rah was the only one left bound in chains waiting for their mercy or blades!

No mercy was shown to traitors in Nazaar's camp and his people showed even worse to his enemies. Rah was beheaded with a blunt sacrificial dagger by Jericho, who was a distant cousin to both kings but a centurion under Nazaar's army. Jericho was one of the few royals who loved king Menelick, and ever since his death he had vowed vengeance on who ever had slain him. He took a vow to kill them slowly but painfully. Rah, true to his nature as a great warrior, never screamed nor cried for mercy but he left them with words that troubled everyone that was there!

Rah: Today you kill me *ngobuthundu begqamu yamazilo kodwa liyeza elenkemba ezodabula izizwe, liyeza!*[59]

So general Rah died and he was buried with his twin sister but they mismatched their heads with the bodies, such that Glenda's body had Rah's head and Rah's body had Glenda's head. This was to mock them even in death but this evil deed was a karma that also sealed their fate. Common men had no right to bury great warriors and legends but even worse, to behead them and mock them! Mockery in death was an outright sin against all deities in the natural and supernatural world.

The punishment was death in both worlds and ending the family lines of the perpetrators but the men had taken a vow to never disclose the secret to anyone! Kane had seen them from afar as he was making his escape!

Back in the centre and hot zone of the battlefield, the war was still largely on. Both sides had lost a plethora of men and even more were injured. It eventually came to a point where a days' war became a months' war with no side wielding or accepting defeat. Everyone was tired and weary and there was a shortage of supply lines to feed and medicate the large hordes of soldiers.

59 With a blunt sacrificial dagger but the day of the sword that will divide nations is coming

The Treaty of Wild Fruits

The first Africans never knew what to call or make of the wild berries and fruits that they used to gather, therefore they were untouched and uneaten until this very day! It was initially thought that trees that bore edible fruits were to be left for the gods such that when the fruits fell or dried up, it was seen as a sign that the gods were enjoying a celestial feast, and the fallen fruits were divine crumbs that would rot and bore seeds. These seeds would then beautify the earth with vegetation and more trees, making the world a beautiful place for both gods and man to dwell in!

People were dying in terrifying numbers at the battle of *Ngulade*. On the other hand, war could not be stopped as this would mean more time to recuperate, recruit, train and feed the troops and this was impossible in a short space of time. On the eve of Friday on the second month of the war, the two brothers met. Both tired and weary of war but they sat 100 metres away from each other, with a few of their trusted warriors accompanying them both.

The communication was simple! Each king was to write whatever they intended to include and address on the treaty and then tie *umhlanga*[60] on a javelin and throw it at the feet of the other king. In response, the other king had to do the same whether he agreed or disagreed with the terms of the treaty until one of the kings got tired. The one who got tired first was to succumb to the terms of the victorious king therefore it was also a test of endurance and power, an ancient form of arm wrestling

Umhlanga was an ancient tablet/plaque made of strong straw that

60   A reed

97

could be folded and tied with a knot to an object such as a spear or javelin and thrown to relay the message to the person that should receive it from a far distance.

Nazaar was the first to throw the javelin and he aimed at directly at his young brother however Theodore got hold of the javelin mid-air and read the terms inscribed by his older brother. It was exactly what he wanted for his camp also but he couldn't just let his bother have the upper hand. He wrote the same terms and threw the javelin right back, at Nazaar but he also caught it mid-air before it stabbed him or any of his subjects!

Nazaar knew very well that his brother had agreed to the terms thus he didn't bother opening the terms, instead he threw the spear right back at Theodore and this cycle continued for a while with neither of the brother backing down. Finally after some time with no outright winner, the custom inducted and allowed the queens to be 'thrown' instead of the javelins. This was to represent their king's intentions and ultimately to fight for the right and honour of their kings.

The two queens had to fight using javelins as the symbol of the agreement, ceremonially appropriate weapon and tool of relaying messages at war. Tahia, the scorpion queen as she was nick-named by the Egyptians arose from Nazaars' camp, dwarfing and towering the lean but athletic Willow from Theodore' camp. This was a fight to the death and both women were amazons compared to other typical women of the various tribes although, Tahia was the vividly larger of the two!

The battle began swiftly between the two women and everything else was dead silent, except the sound emanating from the two female warriors as they fought intensely. Tahia was a master of the sword whilst Willow was an expert of the double head axe, therefore the javelin was breaking new grounds for both of them and it is why the fight took longer than anticipated.

At one point it seemed as if Willow was going to win but the tide would shift as Tahia would scratch or throw her aside like a peach. Whether it was the genesis of the age of extinction of the Bhanda people or just plain bad luck at the time, it is uncertain but what was certain is that this was one of the signs! After a while, both Tahia and Willow got tired and they both knew they had one last shot at killing their opponent. Tahia's plan was to go straight for the heart but because Willow was shorter, she had to gauge the right moment and space to do that.

Willow on the other hand knew that she had to be quicker and round Tahia faster than she could react, she would stab her through the neck and head, partially beheading her in a way to appease her camp and king. So Willow began the attack forward, evading Tahia's javelin very time she attacked her with it until she was in range.

However as she attacked Tahia, Willow hadn't seen that Tahia had also boxed her to the same kill spot that she wanted. Their javelins broke into 2 halves when they bumped onto each other but both women managed to get hold of the nearest piece and stab each other with it, much to the disarray of the spectators.

As they slowly withered into each other's arms, Tahia and Willow embraced each other before finally passing on. This was the birth of the phrase "*caught in arms*" because even if both warriors were enemies, at the end they held each other in respect, honour and most importantly in arms. Everyone was mortified by this sight but the two kings were agrieved.

Both of them had just lost the love of their lives to a conquest of champions and war that they could have avoided easily! They couldn't weep for them nor bury them themselves because whatever died in sacred and peaceful land belonged to the land! They could only watch as the two dead bodies stood kneeling and hugging each other, with javelin tips sticking out of their backs.

This was a true warrior's way to die and it was unique. The place was called *Zindala Zombili*[61] to signify evenness between the two fallen warriors and also to honour the memory of the two great queens! The agreement was sealed, both camps would eat the wild fruits and take whatever they could from the *Ngulade* people and for the coming 2 weeks there was no war. Everyone had to mourn the death of the queens even if they were not buried officially and royally!

Kane on the other hand was hastily making his way up north, as he had been instructed by the fallen general! Everything was blur to him, he couldn't believe that he had seen his people, family and loved ones being executed! How could people be so cruel? None had ever loved him or cared for him like Glenda had and as for Rah, he saw a father he never had in him. They were beginning to get to know each other better but all that had been taken away from him by the Bhanda people, savages he called them!

As he was walking, Kane saw a recently dead rhino carcass but it was surrounded by a pride of lions who were feasting on it. He was hungry but there was no way he could attack a pride of meat-eaters alone! He was still stalking the pride and waiting for his chance for the leftovers, a male lion roared fiercely towards his direction. It had dictated him and came charging at him with all its might.

There was nowhere to run for the young man because he clearly couldn't outpace the king of the jungle. It was now a kill or be killed situation but how could he fight a lion without a weapon? Suddenly he wished he had kept one of the swords or spears that he had tossed

61 They are at par

away along the way. Maybe it was naivety or simple youth but the reality was that he was about to become the pride's next meal if he didn't do something about it!

However as the lion was about to attack him, it unfortunately fell into quick sand, and started to sink as it roared in fear and panic. It doesn't matter what type of specie one is or how strong one can be, everything knows the look and smell of death. The lion felt it, too, one could tell from its wailing roar! In a way, it had saved Kane because he hadn't seen the spot where the quick sand began since it was hidden by the marshy and low bushy area!

The lions seemed not to mind the ordeal that was happening as they were occupied by the feast on the rhino's carcass. Maybe the pride had gone days without eating, and they were extremely famished meaning the less mouths and competition on the food, the better! Kane on the other hand was now faced with a hard choice again. He could live the lion to drown and die or he could try to pull it out by tying a long and strong whip, a weapon and tool that all cowboys and young boys of his age always carried everywhere!

If he was to save the lion, he had to bind its front legs with the longer side of the whip as this would allow him to try and swerve the beast of the jungle to the less muddy part of the puddle! This would drain every ounce of energy he had left and if it succeeded he still had no guarantee that the lions wouldn't devour him after that.

Kane decide to follow his gut feeling and try to save the lion and as destiny would have it, he managed to save it! The lion came out of the quick sand muddy and less ferocious! It was as if it somehow knew that it owed its life to Kane as it showed its gesture of appreciation by scooting down as if it had been instructed too! Kane was lost for words, he couldn't even feel his legs, it was all like a dream but he quickly scooted down also and patted the lion's forehead as it roared loudly!

They were brothers now, friends although different species in every way. As Kane was gearing up to stride along and go on his way, the lion shocked him. It had hastily ran using a safer route back to the carcass and tore a big chunk of meat and brought it back to Kane's feet! This time the whole pride had followed the king, roaring fiercely, to appreciate what the young man had done.

Kane took the meat which was dripping blood and used the blood to write an "S" on the lion's forehead as an abbreviation for Simba the name he gave it. Now this is the story of Simba the lion king *and the genesis of the tale of "umcilo wamakhosikazi" (the rainbow)*. It wasn't about the numerous colours that the rainbow shows vividly, it was about the different character and actions that the pride and their king showed that day, the different colours! Kane quickly went on his journey, continuing to the north as he had been instructed swearing vengeance on the Bhanda people and everyone associated with them.

Back at the battlefield, the mourning period for the two queens had passed and now it was time for the final phase of the war! Just as every other battle before, the war was intense and brutal. One by one, more Bhandas fell to the relentless sword of their own make. There was no mercy or room to waiver, death was the reigning god and the serenades of a warrior's fall and cry when the lifeless bodies thud, hitting the ground, as the spirit left the flesh. The battlefield was quite a site! However, this time there was no room for a stalemate, it ultimately came to the point that everyone dreaded but uniformly needed to decide the fate of the kingdom, the 100 cuts!

100 CUTS

The worst outcome of fear and loathing something in life, multipled by 100, is usually painful or even worse, death! Nazaar had to fight his own blood but not just fighting Theodore to kill him but to slay him with the 100ᵗʰ cut that he would inflict on him!

A human being's body has about 22 crucial pressure points and if handled inappropriately, one may die. Furthermore, there are over 10 main veins and arteries in a human being, if cut or torn, the outcome without immediate help, is another death statistic. This was a duel where one fought, slicing the life out of their opponent with the 100th cut to their body!, As two bulls stabbing each other with horns, running and bumping into each other until one of them yielded through the last to death, this was the current storm.

In this current context, the two brothers were the two bulls facing the same law, stab or cut your opponent for 100 times and inherit the great throne of the Bhanda people. Failure meant death and no one wanted to die with 100 cuts to their body which represented nothing but their ultimate failure as a warrior and *unfit* want to be king!

The stakes were too high for both kings but custom was custom and the elders had willed, and voted for a parlay of the tradition of 100 cuts. This was to save the empire before it was wiped away by a civil war and the final sign to conduct this custom came from the gods! This was done by playing a game called the egg. In this game, the two participants had one thing to do, carry a hot quail's egg in their mouth without letting it fall down or breaking it!

It was a game that was built for its participants to lose for the survival of a larger cause and preservation of a people! Theodore and Nazaar both failed dismally as they couldn't even carry the egg on their hands or better yet fit it in their mouths without breaking it! Their fate was sealed, they were going to be remembered by this fight today no matter what they had done or hoped to achieve. This war had claimed many lives and time and all wanted it to be over, not because they were tired but because they feared Egyptians.

It was making headlines, that they had were invading and conquering everything under the sovereign governance and rule of *Naré Mari*! This is the same man that Rah had tasked Kane to seek before his death. The Egyptians under Pharaoh Naimer were closer than ever to the Bhanda Empire and it was only a matter of days before an inevitable clash would occur. The Bhanda people had to be ready for this and being ready meant having a king and leader to follow to war.

When the collision finally broke out as custom had endorsed, the first cut was drawn by Theodore resurrecting a sleeping beast within Nazaar, who inflicted three rapid and deep cuts to his younger brother! It was real now and all felt it. No one was allowed to speak or even move when kings fought except for the royal singer. This individual was born for one purpose only and that was to sing in all royal occasions, bad or good, painful or splendid and even in burials.

He was the ancient undertaker and poet of death, with his serenades and high notes of either doom or better tomorrows. On such an occasion, this was the worst and probably toughest day of his life because his skills and body would be tested beyond limit. He had to sing until the last cut and one of the kings fell. By the way the fight was going, it wasn't ending any time soon meaning more singing for him!

As the two brothers were still fighting using short range and medium double urged swords called *umdlwedlwebulo*, the royal singer collapsed and died mid-point of a high note. It could have been due to dehydration and excessive abuse of the vocal chords but whatever it was, it halted the brawl for some minutes as all were shocked! They also wondered what that meant. Could it be a sign from the gods?

Up North, Kane was getting nearer to Nare Mari's lands. Nare Mari's scouts had been actually following him from afar, when he was closer to their camp as this was one of their strategy. Unfortunately for them, Simba and the pride killed them all as they were following Kane, also from afar in hiding. When the news broke out of an 'alien' young boy at the gate, the great pharaoh was greatly amused, not because of this update but because the so called alien boy had managed to evade all the traps and his scouts to make it to the gate.

No one had ever made it to the gate, subordinates' agendas and problems were usually dealt with at the bush, by beheading or solving them without bothering the great Pharaoh, with *small things*. Nare Mari was impressed such that he went out barefooted to meet the young Kane at the gate. When they met, Kane was tired and sore from all the long days of walking and blazing heat but Naimer saw him exactly for what he was. Before he even tried to speak, he knew that the young man was a naturally *"born great"* like him.

It didn't matter what skin colour Kane was or how different he was from others, what mattered was that Pharoah Nare Mare adopted him to be one of his sons and named him Maahes, the *lord of slaughter*, because he had heard what had happened in the bush from soothsayers.

Maahes, (Mahes, Mihos, Miysis, Mysis) as he was known, was a solar war god who took the form of a lion. He was a specific god in the Egyptian Kingdom, and he remained fairly obscure. He was of mixed origin, and was an Egyptian version of Apedemak, the lion-god worshipped in Nubia. His name can be translated directly as "one who can see in front." Maahes was rarely referred to by name. Rather he was usually referred to by his most common epithet, "The lord of the Massacre." He was given a num-

ber of other bloodcurdling epithets including; "Wielder of the Knife," "The Scarlet lord," referring to the blood of his victims and "lord of Slaughter." He punished those who violated the rules and promoted order and justice. Thus he was also known as the "Avenger of Wrongs" and "Helper of the Wise Ones."

Lions were closely linked to royalty in Egyptian mythology and Maahes was considered to be the patron of the pharaoh. As such, he was described as the son of Bast, who could take the form of a lion or sand cat. His cult centre was Leontopolis (Nay-ta-hut, "city of lions") in Egypt, where tame lions were lovingly cared for in his temple. Furthermore, he was considered to be the personification of the burning heat of the sun and was also considered to be the guardian of sacred places and a protector of the innocent.

In addition, Maahes was often depicted as a lion-headed man carrying a knife and wearing the Double Crown of Upper and Lower Egypt, the Atef crown or a solar disk and Ureas (royal serpent). Less often, he was depicted as a lion devouring a victim. Nevertheless, god or just pure human, this was just another extension of Kane as the tale goes.

Although Kane could never be fully recognized as an Egyptian or prince, Pharoah Nare Mare sensed an instant connection with him, one he had never felt before, not even with his biological sons.

Kane disclosed everything that had happened to him, not knowing that he had given Nare Mari all the ammunition and information he needed to invade the defragmented Bhanda Empire. That empire threatened the growth of his empire further south of Africa. It was the chance that Egypt had been waiting for all along, to sucker punch the Bhanda people whilst they least expected it and at their weakest point to resist the Egyptian invasion. Quickly, the great Pharaoh rallied his troops for war and marched with them towards the Bhanda lands.

Kane was torn in-between as reality sank in. He had just given his new found family the ammunition to wipe out his tribesmen but he didn't care, everyone had to pay for what they had done to him! Nare Mare promised him the Bhanda throne when he had conquered the empire and in return, the Bhanda Empire would be split into smaller kingdoms under the supervision of Kane as the king. He was however, to pay tribute to Nare Mare to supplement the Egyptian expansion and quest of civilization.

Tracking back to the current date the Bhanda civil war, Nazaar and Theodore were still fighting whilst Nare Mari was moving upon the Bhanda Empire to invade it. On the 50th cut, the brothers were a tie. They could barely move due to the loss of blood. Puddles of their blood had been formed on the ground.

King Nazaar: You know they like it brother, that we are entertaining them for once!

King Theodore: It's a shame that when this is allover, all they will remember of the fallen is that he lost not his legacy, not his beautiful state captured wives, daughters and yes, the ones they will kill first, his sons! We are the born great but dead young, big brother! Royalty is shadowed greed with gold ornaments and shiny tyranny that the common ones will always be subdued under! Everything is vanity!

King Nazaar: I agree brother, but today we have foolishly allowed custom to wipe us all out and I promise you, this sand shall bear testimony to our demise and no one shall remember that we were the Bhanda!

Our bones shall dry and our history with them. A great flood comes from the north but we are not ready. We have fought a great fight you and I, since childhood brother and I always beat you (*both chuckle*) but what comes next doesn't matter who we are and what we were! The enemy will strike before dawn as he has already laid siege on us whilst we have been squabbling for power and cresting ourselves for the biggest and largest ego to be heard and seen. You should die for what you did but I will always be your big brother and I love you even if you are taller than me (*both laugh and shed a tear*). We both know what must be done now!

King Theodore: Make it quick dear brother and make it hurt! I love you too.

As the brothers got up and embraced each other in one last, long, sweaty and bloody hug, Theodore fell on his knees and kissed his brothers feet and then looked at him for the last time. He looked back at his family and gestured with his head for Nazaar to do it! Nazaar slashed Theodore with the quickest 49 cuts ever and on the last one to complete the 100 cuts, they were drawn in an eye contact with his young brother as he was weeping like a child, with mucus and blood covering his body.

King Theodore: Remember my king, it's all on you now, they need you more than ever, protect them and rule well!

| King Nazaar: | Die well brother! |
| | (*Nazaar said these words as he unleashed the finally cut, which was actually a stab rather to the heart to quicken his brother's death and save him from pain…*) |

"All hail king Nazaar," the whole of the Bhanda kingdom roared, even Nare Mari and his desert cogs could hear it but Nazaar was broken that day. Theodore was his nemesis but he was also his brother, and that love and bond shattered his soul to pieces even though it had to be done. The survival of the Bhanda Empire rested on this reality and both he and Theodore knew very well that there was a larger purpose and threat to the kingdom, than a civil war.

Theodore's death was a sacrifice for the greater good of the empire as the Bhanda people needed to be unified under one king, in order to have a chance against the new and big threat. Theodore was honoured and recognised as a hero and king at his brother's command in his funeral. He was laid next to their father, and for the first time in the Bhanda kingdom, the general public were given a choice to accompany the king to the afterlife. On that day, a thousand virgin girls and boys broke their necks, to accompany and attend to the dead king in the afterlife.

King Nazaar even allowed Theodore's sons and family to bury their father, which wasn't the usual custom but he knew that great sacrifices came with new beginnings, and this was a start of many to come. This might have seemed noble and to a point humane but the god's were not happy with Nazaar, as he had broken every vow of vengeance he had made against his brother. That included the stab on the custom of 100 cuts, he had broken the law sacrilegiously in their sight!

Nature has only one punishment for a king and that is unfortunately, death and his was surely coming! As the Bhanda people gathered for a war of their very own existence under their new king, after the mourning period had elapsed, a rumble was heard all over the land. Trees shook, birds stopped singing and no one dared make a sound. It was like everybody knew what was going to happen and who was going to make it all happen. The only word that everyone heard from the trumpets and drums when they began to be played with intense gusto, as the elephants charged forward breaking the boundary walls, followed by an Egyptian army that dwarfed the Bhanda people in a scale of 10:1 was Nare Mari!

The Legend of Naré Mari – The First Pharoah

Naré Mari was a true African legend and the first Pharaoh of the first dynasty. He founded the unified Egypt that ruled the world for years and years. About 300,000 years ago in the regions called *Ta Ntjer* in ancient Egypt, meaning *God's own land*. The *Anu* people, who were some of the first human beings, migrated from the Great lakes, through the Nile to Sudan, where they invented Agriculture, together with some of the tribes such as the Bhanda people.

In Sudan, they built the first stone city and originated the Pharaonic civilization. From Sudan, the Anu people went further down the Nile to Egypt where they built more cities, the Great Sphinx and the renowned pyramids. Furthermore, the Delta of Northern Egypt was formed when minerals from the holy regions of the Great Lakes were washed down by the river. The settling of the *Kamtiu* (Egyptians) on the Delta was brief because White Asians invaded the Delta, and the *Kamtiu* had to go back.

This led to several wars and struggle for the Delta between the Northern foreigners and the Southern Kings. In order to take the Delta once and for all, and unify the Southern and Northern regions, the kings of *Nehkhab, Abju, Nubet, Yeb* and *Nekhen*, came together in *Nagaba* and chose Naré Mari, King of Nekhen as the most relevant Southern King to conquer the Delta.

Meni Horo Naré Mari Tjau was born to Queen Sesh and King Serkhet Horo Ka, not long after the invention of writing, years ago. So he was established in the civilizational and historical awareness of his roots, and this could be seen in his artistic illustrations of his escapades. The unification of Egypt is illustrated on Naré Mari's tablet, a big stone that was used by artist for art, which is still preserved in the Cairo Museum.

Naré Mari began by eliminating blacks who were resistant to Pharaonic authority and conquered the land, after which he wore the *Hedjet*, which is the white crown of Southern Egypt. This included tribes such the Bhanda. He further conquered Lower Egypt by eliminating the white Asians. This can be seen on his tablet as he wore the *Desheret* (the red crown of Northern Egypt) and holds the *Nekhasha* (the fly whisk) in his right hand; this was deemed to allow him to cast out evil spirits. All these are illustrated on his tablet.

He was bestowed with the titles; *Henu Shemau Mehu* (Northern and Southern Sovereign), *Nsut Bity* (The Southern King who conquered the North), and *Neb Tawy* (Master of both lands). He was the first to wear both crowns. Naré Mari's reign was marked with Egypt's militarization, he created the *Men Nafooré*, (Memphis), between Upper Egypt and Lower Egypt and fortified it to prevent further assault. The city was named after his name (*Menes*). Memphis became the capital city of Northern or Lower Egypt, while *Nekhen* remained the capital of Southern Egypt. He reinforced his authority in Gaza, which was then inhabited by fellow Blacks, the *Kin-anu* people (The Canaanites).Naré Mari handed down a powerful, unified Egypt to his successors who grew Egypt into the world power that ruled the world for 3,000 years, civilizing Asia, America, and Europe. In West Africa, the names Naré and Mari are still used till date, in Mali and Burkina Faso. A famous example is Sundjata Keita, the founder of the Mali Empire; his father was Naré Maghan Konate, while he was called Mari Djata Keita. The name Mari means *loved* in the Pharaonic language and some believe it is the origin of the Christian name Mary.

CHAPTER FOUR

(KINGS AND QUEENS)

When the invasion began, Kane was seated on top of a royal camel, an animal that was not known or seen around Bhanda land. For those that saw him at a glance before their ultimate demise, they finally saw him as the king he was born to be. He had long and coiled Rastafarian braided like hair that touched his elbows every time he moved or swayed. Under the Egyptians, life had totally changed for him. He was someone, loved, respected and most importantly, a king's son!

At the time of this ancient civilization, there were vast languages just as today but uniquely everyone knew, heard and respected what the other group meant or alluded to when they spoke or gestured in a certain way, and that is where the idea or myth of *one blood and one Africa comes from*. It didn't matter that some tribes were inferior, what mattered was to understand and listen to the implications of a particular ethnic dialect, because that was the key of starting and winning every war! Secrets, slang and all types of military and social basic confidentialities predate the very existence of writing itself. And Kane was the Bhanda Empire's Achilles' heel!

Maahes as Kane was known by to the Egyptians, told them everything from the basic stuff to the most complex. It was a fight that the Bhanda were bound to lose as the Egyptians knew how to mirror their every move. Out of all the battles that the Bhanda had fought and won flawlessly, this war with the Egyptians eradicated everything they had fought for and stood for as an empire. Some have alluded to this war as the first "*Mfecane/Lifaqane/Difaqane*"[62] war but the truth is that this was something more.

There was no *Madlantule*[63] famine to trigger it, or countless small tribes battling for territory and wealth. This was a war that defined the age of expansion and the spread of civilization in the whole of Africa, the "*Mantengwane*[64] war!" This was the genesis of the today songs of praises we sing to support teams such as Highlanders which is also known as *Cry Mantengwane*, in Zimbabwe was the capital city of the Bhanda Empire.

The Mantengwane War

When the Egyptian mammoths broke the Great green wal, the first Bhanda tribe to face them where then Dahomey Amazons. The ancient Great green wall was a fortified wall of clustered and strong trees such as the Baobab. It was the first defensive measure for the Bhanda Empire and for centuries, no one had ever breached it until now!

The same wall also known as Great Green Wall of the Sahara and the Sahel, is Africa's flagship initiative to combat the effects of desertification. Led by the African Union, the initiative aims to transform the lives of millions of people, by creating a mosaic of green and productive

62 Crushing, scattering, forced dispersal, forced migration

63 suffer hunger but do not speak

64 The bird of prey which terrorises other birds which resonates well with the stereotype of the Bhanda Empire as violent and imperialists bent on destroying and destabilizing African peace.

landscapes across Africa. From the initial idea of a line of trees from east to west bordering the African desert, the vision of a Great Green Wall has evolved into that of a mosaic of interventions addressing the challenges facing the people in the Sahel and the Sahara. As a programming tool for rural development, the overall goal of this partnership is to strengthen regional resilience and natural systems with sound ecosystem management, protection of rural heritage, and improved living conditions.

The project is a response to the combined effect of natural resources degradation and drought in rural areas. It is a partnership that supports communities working towards sustainable management and use of forests, rangelands and other natural resources. It seeks to help communities mitigate and adapt to climate change, as well as improve food security. The Sahel's population is expected to double by 2039, adding urgency to the project.

However when the Dahomey Amazons faced the Egyptian hordes in all their might, they were quickly brushed aside by their mighty foe! The Dahomey Amazons were a Fon women-only military regiment in the Kingdom of Dahomey, which is nowadays' Republic of Benin, which was a colony of the Bhanda empire. The Dahomey Amazons, also known as Mino, which translates as 'our mothers', were very well trained to become ferocious fighters and they had the reputation of decapitating their foe right in the middle of battles. Moreover, Bhanda kings used to seek their immaculate skill as torturers to those who didn't become their captives.

The Egyptians managed to capture Seh-Dong-Hong-Beh, who was their famous leader and has the untainted legacy of leading an army of 6,000 women against an Egyptian army that outmatched their numbers astronomically. Despite the fact that the Dahomey Amazons fought with swords, spears, and bows, only about 1,200 of them survived this battle, because of Naimer's superior warfare and military prowess with the use of telluric iron and the chariot.

The Telluric iron Age saw the development of telluric iron weapons, which featured sharper cutting edges than other weapons made out of stone, bronze and other materials. The discovery of telluric iron had an important impact on warfare. Telluric Iron weapons were forged, not cast like bronze, so that they were less brittle and more reliable than earlier weapons made from bronze. Furthermore, unlike bronze, which required hard-to-find tin to produce, telluric iron was widely available, allowing armies to obtain a plentiful supply of inexpensive weapons.

Combined with such an invention was a major advance in combat when the bow and arrow, the wheel, and the domesticated horse were combined to create the war chariot. For the first time soldiers could advance on a position in a surprise attack, deliver a deadly javelin or arrow attack from a mobile platform, and quickly race away to regroup or engage in lethal pursuit of a terrified and broken foe. Chariot-borne warriors were the elite strike force of the Egyptian army and gave Egypt a tactical advantage over its opponents. Sophisticated war machines such as the catapult also gave the Egyptians a decisive advantage against their opponents and helped them spread civilization all over the world.

Nazaar understood that in order to have a chance to evade the Egyptian invasion, he had to deploy the *"batsira avo vanokubatsira*[65]*"* policy were he allied himself with tribes that took an oath of allegiance to him. Tribes such as the Dahomey Amazons and Biriwa amongst others had revolted against him, hence they were to face the Egyptian

65 Help those that help you

might alone. If the Bhanda managed to win the war, such tribes would be totally wiped out of the face of the earth, and unfortunately such a scenario wasn't to be as the second Bhanda tribe to fall to the Egyptian might was the Biriwa tribe. This was one of the largest Bhanda tribes that is located in modern day Sierra Leone.

The Biriwa tribe was led by Almamy Suluku who was a smart, powerful Limba ruler who managed to maintain and prolong the war for a long time. He became war captain of Northern Bhanda tribes, a position that was good as deputy general of the Empire. The Biriwa, had learned fast from the Dahomean war that an open and fully fledged war against the Egyptians would be an inevitable slaughter therefore they sought alliance with other Northern Bhanda tribes such as Ndongo and Matamba.

Ndongo and Matamba tribes that were led by Nzinga. She was a powerful and smart ruler of the Ndongo and Matamba tribes (nowaday's Angola) of the Mbundu people. The combined force of by Almamy Suluku of the Biliwa, Nzinga of Ndongo and Matamba and Amina of Zaria Emirate wisely and fearlessly fought against the Egyptians for freedom. Nzinga had built her army by offering sanctuary to runaway slaves and mercenaries and then started working on developing Matamba as a trading power as well as a gateway to Central Africa's interior.

She had transformed Matamba into a powerful tribe that, throughout the time, resisted several Egyptian colonization attempts. Queen Amina or Aminatu on the other hand, was a warrior queen of the Zaria Emirate Bhanda tribe, which is in modern day Nigeria. She was the subject of many legends since she had managed to conquer many cities and ruled for 34 years before the Bhanda Empire finally defeated and assimilated her kingdom into the Bhanda Empire. She was a legendary and eager warrior, and as a child her grandmother found her wielding a dagger as nimbly as any warrior. Furthermore, she refused to marry so that she would not risk losing any authority. One of her less fearsome legacies is that she introduced the cultivation of kola nuts to her kingdom.

As the Clash with the Egyptians finally took course in the northern region of Bhanda land, Amina and Nzinga and Almamy Suluku's troops were divided into companies and regiments, each with their own unique emblem. Designated field commanders controlled troop movement with signals from drums, bells and elephant tusk horns. Unlike the Dahomeans, the archers of the "*seleka*" (meaning coalition in Sango language) of the 3 rebel Bhanda tribes opened the battle with a very high volley of arrows whilst hiding from tree tops. The main force was the unit of spear and swordsmen who were deployed systematically by a "*mutungamiri simba*" (strong leader) chosen when the strongest, bravest and wisest warriors of all three tribes fought and the victor earned the title and command.

Deployment was staggered, so that initial fighting waves fell back on command when tired, and fresh contingents moved up from the rear to take their place. However this tactic was okay for a foot war and for a small scale battle but was not even a scratch in the back for the military prowess of Naimer's forces. Like the Dahomeans before, the seleka was crushed with Almamy Suluku fleeing down south to the Bhanda capital in Mantengwane were the entire Bhanda might was stationed and ready for war. Queen Amina and Nzinga were unfortunately captured and faced exile in Egypt until the end of their days.

When Almamy Suluku barged into the capital injured and weak from the Egyptian conflict. Laibon Mbatian of the Masai Bhanda tribe, Xhii of the San Bhanda tribe, Mwapo of the Hadza Bhanda tribe,

Lipumbu Ya Tshilongo of the Nama Bhanda tribe, Barmandana of the Pene and Malal Bhanda tribes and Kunanyi of the Palawa Bhanda tribe all wanted to finish him off. They saw him as a traitor and all traitors were treated with great ill in the Bhanda lands, However, King Nazaar had learned from his past experiences that sometimes your greatest ally is also your enemy therefore he ordered everyone to stand down and the physicians to attend to the wounded Almamy Suluku. When Almamy Suluku had captured his breathe, the king then asked him, the only question that mattered at the time.

King Nazaar: Tell me dear brother, what comes and goes like the wind but stays stagnant like the rotten stench of unscaled tuna fish?

Almamy Suluku: Lies ooh great king, lies! (*Looking down embarrassed*)

King Nazaar: Stand on your feet brother, you will kneel for a king that has earned your respect! These are not the times of squabbles or grudges but this is a time of great peril and pain. You have seen them, battled them and here you are... broken and lost... So I ask you again brother, what comes and goes like the wind but stays stagnant like the rotten stench of unscaled tuna fish?

Almamy Suluku: Egyptian scum brother, those filthy Egyptian pigs!

119

King Nazaar:	Good brother. Good! Remember all....

Almamy Suluku:	And forgive none! Your Father used to say that! I am sorry that I and my people deserted you at this pressing time of need mighty king but from now on, I pledge my allegiance to you. Please show mercy and allow the Biriwa tribe to fight as Bhanda warriors again. The enemy rides swiftly and kills in impeccable frightening valour. I watched my people's lives being clawed out of their helpless bodies one by one by the Egyptian sword and let me tell you my king, these men are not common men! It's like they have fought us before and conquered us and now they are just back to finish us off!

King Nazaar:	Tell me more about this Nare Mari... the one those rats call Pharoah!

Almamy Suluku:	It is unfortunate that I didn't get the chance to see him my king as the battle was intense. But I fear the young warrior prince they called Maahes because he slew more of my people using his bare hands in an excruciating way that I have never seen before. Rumour has it that he is one of ours, a Bhanda....a bastard Prince! Analbinomy king!

King Nazaar:	The gods have surely come to punish us for a culture they ordained us to follow! I heard a tale

once that my father had sired a bastard son with a common harlot but I never really took it serious since we never heard of him all these years! So we killed him and now he kill us... what a shame to be king! Tell me then of my *"mutorwa"* (alien) brother... does the warrior blood flow in him?

Almamy Suluku: He reminds me of a young Nazaar! Thirsty for blood and restless for the next kill! He may be with them my king but he breezes through his opponents as they fall like a seamless Bhanda whirlwind! If I can speak plainly great king..!

King Nazaar: Speak!

Almamy Suluku: I have never been scared or moved by anything or anyone all my life and I say that in the most humble and respectable way to the great king! But Maahes scares me! He reeks of an uncommon aurora and evil that can only be quenched by dark magic and blood my king! They say he doesn't know how to fight only but he was trained by Glenda the horrible, the great witch we beheaded at the Ngulade!

King Nazaar: In all the years of my life, I have sought a worthy opponent and person to pass the torch to! Theodore has always been the closest but his gone now! If Maahes seeks retribution and the throne

121

then will the gods forgive me yet again for spilling another brother's blood? We are victims of a royal custom you and I Almamy Suluku and we are the only ones that understand what must be done! I forgive you brother and accept your allegiance but remember,"Nce o etsa qeto, bokahohle bo rela no etsa hore e etsahale"[66]

So the Bhanda braced themselves for the most epic and timeless battle of their life under the shrewd Intel of Almamy Suluku who had faced the Egyptians before and saw their might! The Bhanda Empire comprised of many ethnic tribes that included, the San, Nama, Sandawe, Hadza, Palawa, Masaai, the Pene and Malal amongst other notable Bhanda tribes.

Maasai

Today the Maasai are one of the most internationally famous African tribes that still exist. The tribe was known for its vibrant outfits and distinct customs as it is even up to now. Observing and visiting the Maasai people is one of the most popular tourist's attractions in Kenya but a few know about their core history. Laibon Mbatian was the first Maasai Bhanda leader who ensured that the tribe was known for its warriors, who were feared for throwing "orinka" (clubs) over 100 meters (328 feet). The Masai also wore intimidating headdress called the "Enkuwaru" made of ostrich plumes worn for hunting lions and luck in war.

66 Once you have made a decision, the universe conspires to make it happen.

They also possessed shields that were made of buffalo hide and decorated with natural vegetable dyes. Shields remain one of the Maasai warrior's most important tools. They were used in warfare and hunting as well as practice and training. Outside of the warring context, however, shields were used in rites of passage and also functioned as prestige objects and symbols of identification. Younger warriors were only allowed the use of black, white, or grey on their shields, indicating that the shield was owned by a proven warrior herder.

Amongst the most famous Maasai traditions is the "adamu" (jumping dance), the wearing of colorful "shuka", spitting and the drinking of blood. The vibrant coloured cloth worn by the Maasai is known as shuka. Red is considered to be a sacred colour and represents blood and is the basic colour for all shuka. In addition to these qualities, it also protects the Maasai from wild animals. Orange is for hospitality, warmth and friendship, blue is for the sky which provides the rains for the cattle.

Green is nourishment and production and yellow is for fertility and growth. Together, these vibrant African clothes, are what made the Maasai so distinctive in Africa. The "adamu" on a different note is the jumping dance which is performed as part of the initiation right when young adults become men. Accompanied by song, pairs of men take turns to see who can jump the highest. The ritual is performed to show prowess and fitness and it forms a part of the celebration when the boys become eligible bachelors. He who jumps the highest attracts the best bride.

While most African traditions treated the spitting of saliva as a strictly private and personal matter, in Maasai culture and tradition it was considered extremely good luck to be shared. When shaking the hand of an elder, it was important to spit in one's palm and to ward off evil spirits, one had to spit onto a new-born babies head. Spitting was one thing, drinking blood completely another. The Maasai were and still are hematophages, meaning that they drink blood for nourishment.

It is curious because while they drink cow's blood, often mixed with milk, they are opposed to eating wild animals, and the consumption of beef is reserved for special occasions only. The Maasai revere their cattle and for this reason, the letting of blood causes no lasting harm to their cattle.

San (Bushmen)

The San tribe was and still is the oldest African tribe and the world's most ancient race. The San had the most diverse and distinct DNA than any other indigenous African group meaning that they are direct descendants of the original ancestral human groups. Xhii was their leader that wasn't elected by the tribe but by the Bhanda king for his profound expertise of the bow and arrow. The San unlike other tribes didn't have an outright hierarchy of power but the elders were responsible for ensuring that all cultural norms and traditions were upheld.

Even more amazing, was the level of endurance and skill the San possessed in battle for a hunting and gathering time. The San were one of the few tribes that used poisoned arrows at war and they always prayed for their enemies before they killed them as a sign of honour for the life they gave away in order for the San tribe to survive in their stead. At one of the previous battles under king Menelick, Xhii killed 40 men by getting close and shooting them with the poisonous arrows, running away and repeating that again and again until all 40 were dead.

This was where the common African idiom of *"kwabo kwagwala akulasililo"*[67] also came from. The idiom warns people to avoid danger and death as much as possible and also to let violence and confrontation to be the last resort.

Sandawe

The Sandawe lived in modern day central Tanzania near another old African tribe, the Hadza. Like the Hadza and San, the Sandawe speak one of the few remaining click languages in Africa. Furthermore the Sandawe are also descendants of the first humans and shared a common ancestor with the San tribe. They had a variant gene for melanin, which affects skin colour and this made them some of the lightest skinned indigenous African tribes, similarly to the San.

The gods of the Sandawe were activated by an erotic dance called *"phekumo"* in which the act of love was mimicked in embrace by the dancers. This dance embedded the necessity for human and earth fertility in the body, mind and spirit of the dancers as they also pleaded with the gods to save them and their families in war. Due to their face tattoos, the Sandawe were known as the African clowns because they could kill their foes whilst smiling as if nothing had happened. The more tattoos a warrior had, the more his prestige grew.

Unlike other Bhanda tribes, the Sandawe did not believe that iron weapons were meant for war, therefore they used a spiked wooden cudgel in war made from the strongest tree stems at the time. Nyaturu, their leader trained his warriors to always hit their opponents' head first in order to avoid exposure as the Sandawe only wore *"hika"* grass, feathers and hides as both traditional clothing and armour. This was largely

---

67 There is no grief at the home of a coward.

to kill the enemy fast and also protect the Sandawe warrior against a prolonged hand to hand combat against an enemy that carried an iron made weapon such as a sword for example.

Hadza

The Hadza tribe of Hadzabe were and are one of the last true hunter-gatherers. They never grew any crops or kept livestock, and they never had any permanent shelters. Moreover the Hadza spoke a click language called "Hadzane" that was and still is unrelated to any other existing language on Earth. When hunting or gathering, the Hadza can mimic any bird like sound and this is how they get honey and "watch tower" like intel from fowls of the ai,r about any potential dangers that might seek to harm them from afar distance.

Mwapo their leader used to search for honey and big prey using the wits and serenades of a "tik'iliko bird (honey guide bird) and a grey African parrot called Zanzu, intelligent and cunning like in the "Simba the Lion King" movie but realistically! Zanzu wasn't just a talking and clever parrot, Zanzu represented the priceless epitome of a cultural bond and dialect that existed between mankind and other species.

The Hadza believed that this bird was a demigod that guided and taught them a lot of things about the wild and their surroundings. When it came to war, the Hadza didn't just stop at killing their enemies. They harvested whatever they could salvage from their enemies' corpses for making medicine and other health related operations. In fact, the Hadza opted to prolong the death of their enemies so that they could "operate" them for delicate and special organs whilst they were fresh and working!

Palawa

The Palawa were widely known for their small stature, and they also like the other early African Bhanda tribes, descended from some of the earliest groups of humans. Tasmanians or Black Aborigines as they are sometimes called, the Palawa had a different pattern of growth, which accounts for their smaller size. They were born average sized, but grew slowly in early childhood. Some tribes used to mock them that their short stature was a result of malnutrition not the environment and genetics.

They were also known for their curled hair, which was often tiedand complexion which ranged from black to reddish-brown. One of their most prominent features was their broad noses, wide mouths, and sets of deep brown eyes, which gave them an ancient and medieval look and the nick name, "Black Aborigines." They were not pygmies but they were short, and some of them could easily be passed for pygmies, with their little body fat, which made them plump. In war, this tribe was the back-bone of strategy and wisdom as they were naturally wise and peaceful. They were one of the cleverest tribes that could probably challenge the Egyptian might in mathematics and strategy.

Their leader was the shortest of them all but the wisest man in all of the Bhanda Empire and his name was Kunanyi, meaning "mountain" in the Palawa kani language. Kunanyi believed that a man was already conquered if the only weapon he brought to war was size and strength in numbers! To him, everything could be calculated and manipulated to favourable odds as long as people believed that they could achieve it.

He knew that his tribe wasn't braced for war and power due to unbreakable cultural beliefs at the time but he foresaw a future where everyone was equal and offered different abilities to theworld. All that he saw in a dream, and when he woke up, he spoke the wisest words that no one had ever spoken at the time "*nnukwu ihe na-aba na obere ngwugwu*[68]," and so began the Palawa saying up to this very day!

Nama

The Nama are the last true descendants of the Khoikhoi, who are closely related to the San. Today, very few pure Nama people exist because of intermarriage with other tribes and a smallpox outbreak in the 18th century. The Nama were cattle farmers and they called themselves the "Khoikhoi" to distinguish themselves from the rest of the Khoisan Bhanda tribes. Since they were wanderers and gatherers, the Nama lived in huts called "Haru Oms" that were constructed to be easily dismantled and moved elsewhere when they migrated to greener pastures.

The land belonged to everyone in the Nama tradition and their culture was passed down from generation to generation, true immaculate oral tradition. Nama people were the undisputed experts of traditional music, folktales, proverbs, poems and riddles. Lipumbu Ya Tshilongo of the Ovambo clan was their king and he also ruled over Uukwambi territory. He was nicknamed "*Ndilimani*[69]" because he fought a leopard to the death, and lost three of his left hand fingers when he was just an adolescent.

Ndilimani ruled his tribe with an iron fist and many of his enemies fled from his presence or took their own lives, before they even met their judgment. Due to his hard core nature and character as a leader, he revolutionized his soldiers to emulate him. The Nama war-

68 Dynamite comes in small packages
69 Destroyer

riors counted killing 10 enemies as one, because they believed in totally wiping out their enemies. If a young warrior wanted to make a name for himself, he had to kill at least 5 enemies in battle and 5 meant 50 people according to the Nama body count at the time.

Pene and Malal

The Pene and Malal Bhanda tribes were led by the great Barmandana and they lived in large organized settlements near Djenné, one of West Africa's oldest cities. Unlike the other Bhanda tribes, the Pene and Malal tribes had grown and risen as powerful states due to budding trade routes that had shifted southward to the savanna, stimulating the growth of states. Barmandana was a warrior-prince of the Udoka dynasty who was called upon by his people and the gods through mysticism to free the Pene and Malal people from the rule of the king of the Gao Empire, Sudoku Kanté.

Many people today know the sudoku puzzle game made by the Japanese for the amusement and fair pleasure of the global world but the real Sudoku was a despotic and barbaric Gao king. On the day of his eventual demise, Barmandana slew him vertically and horizontally from the waist down and up using an Akrafena sword called the "*Mponponson*[70]" that he had forged himself for that specific purpose. Furthermore, he made a game called *Sudoku*[71] from the bones of Sudoku Kante. This eventually initiated the practice of bone throwing and reading that "*Sangomas and Nyangas*[72]" went on to do and use even up to know.

70`   Meaning responsibility

71   Meaning the parts shall appear once

72   Witch doctors, traditional herbalist and healers

Moreover, the Pene and Malal Bhanda tribes were gifted storytellers known as griots that maintained a strict tradition of oral history of the Bhanda Empire in all the vastness and might. This in modern day times means, these two tribes were the "Google "of the entire Bhanda Empire's history and the Bhanda king always gave them special preference because of this particular and precious skill set. In war, under their great leader, the Pene and Malal tribes were the gurus and initiates of modern day guerrilla warfare. They believed in systematically killing the enemy through stealth, coordinated and hidden attacks that often caught the enemy off-guard and sometimes even surprised them to an extent that they were nicknamed *ogbu mmadu*.[73]

So it was that these Bhanda tribes under the absolute authority and régime of Nazaar that made up the indomitable Bhanda war machine/army and empire. No one had ever conquered the Bhanda Empire ever since its dawn. The Bhanda were relentless people that breathed, ate and spoke "war." At the pinnacle of the Bhanda Empire, it covered more than a quarter of central, west, eastern and southern Africa to a point that if the Bhanda sneezed, the whole of Africa caught the flue except Egypt! When the Egyptian hordes finally made it to the capital being led by Nare Mare, Nazaar finally saw what had made a great warrior like Almamy Suluku to doubt himself and be scared.

Tunka Manin the ruler and accomplished warrior of Ga'na clan of the Wagadou Bhanda tribe ran straight at Nare Mare with an assegai and sword, in a feat to end him and the battle. However Nare Mare did the unthinkable and instructed his soldiers to make way for him, and actually open the space so that everyone could see what would happen. Tunka Manin was a lover of justice and he settled many disputes within

73 Assassins

his tribe personally. He was famous for his involvement in communities and for the fact that he greatly boosted the economy of the Bhanda Empire with gold.

He was a warrior that was able to further cultivate his public image through projecting an air of magic and mysticism. Unfortunately, Tunka Manin was the last ruler of the Wagadou Bhanda tribe as Nare Mari killed him before he could even lift and use his weapons. It was a quick jab, stab and press on his Adam's ample with the thumb. Everyone was shocked when a great warrior like Tunka Manin fell down dead like that!

Both Nazaar and Nare Mare knew very well that a statement of intent had been made and if the Bhanda weren't sacred before, they were running a mile for their lives subconsciously by now! What made it worse was that Nare Mare didn't just kill Tunka Manin and stop there, he took his assegai and sword and carved out his heart and ate it raw whilst his army roared and rallied behind him! That was a moment when the Bhanda were lost of words! King Nazaar knew that he had to make a statement also in order to boost the confidence of his troops therefore he removed his amour and left his weapons at the feet of Changamire Dombo.

Changamire Dombo

He was the leader of the Rozvi Bhanda tribe. He had the military prowess that was second to Nazaar, only in the Bhanda Empire and he was the new general of a new regime in the empire after Rah and Theodore's regime. What made him exceptional was that even though many Bhanda warriors and leaders exhibited great military achievements, Changamire Dombo founded a tribe while simultaneously extinguishing the power and influence of a foreign force in the region.

While the Bhanda Empire was dwindling away largely due to succession disputes and civil unrest, local Shona Bhanda rulerswith wealth had begun developing their own armies.

The most successful of these rulers was Changamire Dombo and he had developed the most ruthless army called the Rozwi or Rozvi, literally meaning destroyers. King Nazaar and Changamire were not only close friends but brother's in-law as Changamire had taken his sister Queen Nondindwa as wife!

His army became a major force in the northeast plateau of Madzimabwe, where he had swallowed up the Mutapa Empire, gaining autonomy in the region, and this was the man that King Nazaar now called brother!

When Nazaar had stripped his entire armour, and left his weapons with his most trusted general, he instructed the guards to open the gate as he strode outside to meet the Egyptians, alone. Many of his chiefs and trusted advisors shouted at him to come back. Some went even further by insulting him, in an attempt to change his mind than suffer a sudden death, before the actual war had even began. He ignored them all even though it was treason to insult the king and the punishment was death. Nazaar understood his people's worry was based on their care and love for him.

This was war and legends were made out of risks that only legends of the same order, will and mind set could understand. Narmer being a great philosopher and warrior king himself, understood exactly what the Bhanda king wanted, and he obliged fully to his desire just to see what his opponent was made of. What Nazaar was doing was called *isiko lokuphuma.*[74] This law was done by a king or queen who was 100% sure that it didn't matter if he orshe died or lived, because the legacy would still live on, due to the love and respect that history would probably have for the,. Most kings who took this initiative had died prematurely because it could make a legend out of someone or a complete fool but either way, the greatest danger was that if the king fell prematurely then the empire would inevitably be next!

Isiko Lokuphuma (The act of Going Out)

This was an act of facing the enemy head on with any weapon, shield or amour hoping that the enemy would grant you leniency and fairness by allowing you to fight his best warrior, or beast and even himself if it came to that. It was an act of hard core guts and steel nerves! History hadn't been kind to all the kings and queens who had tried it before, as all of them had been killed or worse, embarrassed in front of their subordinates!

Narmer however was a different man, he wanted Nazaar to succeed actually so that when he finally met him in person, he would be a worthy opponent for him to kill and bath in his blood in honour of "*Montu.*"[75] So when Nazaar was outside of the capital walls at the mercy of the Egyptian Pharaoh and his army, Narmer ordered Kane to set free the gaur so that everyone could see what the famous and undisputed Bhanda warrior king was made of!

---

74 The act of going out
75 An Egyptian falcon-god of war

Gaur, Seledang

The gaur was the largest, dark-coated wild cow bigger than the African buffalo, the extinct Aurochs, the ancestor of domestic cattle), wild water buffalo or bison and it was also called *seladang*. They were the heaviest and most powerful of all wild cattle, and were among the largest living land animals; only elephants, rhinos, and hippos grew larger. Due to their formidable size and power, the gaur had few natural enemies. Saltwater crocodiles and leopards, but only a tiger could kill a full-grown adult and vice versa. Pharaoh Narmer had gotten hold of some on a voyage and conquest in Asia and his pet god tiger "*Mafdet*[76]," was killed by a gaur.

It was gored and trampled to death by a gaur during a prolonged battle at the Egyptian coliseum in Memphis. The tiger's carcass was further broken down by being fatally struck against the arena's large wall, for the amusement of the eager spectators who paid large sums of money to enjoy such luxuries by a large gaur! This spectacle gave rise to the worship of the gaur and it was given the title of Egyptian goddess, *Hathor* meaning house of Horus. When alarmed, provoked or coerced, the gaur crashed into the jungle or onto the "enemy" at a surprising speed and force, and this was the beast that Narmer was instructing Kane too let loose upon Nazaar! If it struck him, it would be a sudden death on impact and the gaur usually won its duels, with death as its ultimate prize and gift to its master.

So as instructed by his father and Pharoah, Kane ordered some soldiers to release the gaur from its cage that, Narmer called *Insuku*

76 She who runs swiftly

zokuduma[77] because of the sheer rage and thunder-like power that the cage inhabited and the abuse it took as the gaur frequently head-butted it from the interior, trying to get out! When the gaur came out, the cage was faced towards Nazaar, near the entrance of the gate, therefore the first person it saw was the enemy! As tradition had it, all its enemies kissed the ground goodbye before their bodies could even register that they were dying, and bleeding from the gaur's forceful hit!

Nazaar had killed *uMahambayedwa* before but the gaur was a different fight. He knew very well that he could only pray that the gods had found favour in him because if not, he was going to be nailed on to the horns of a raging bull, that wanted nothing more in the world than to end his life. The bull huffed and puffed scraping the ground and stomping the land to the amusement and support of the Egyptians, including the great Narmer himself!

"Maak hom dood dood hy die dier hy staan by die poort van 'n Koninkryk wat ons sal wees[78]*"* sang the Egyptians as the gaur charged at Nazaar. Nazaar had no weapon, amour or the time to evade the attack but he had his heart and wits that had always set him apart from other people. As the gaur got closer to him, Nazaar realised that his red velvet *"kanga/leso"* was loose and so he instinctively undressed and held it like a flag sideways, such that when the gaur came charging, it made a terrible first time miss of both him and the red *Kanga*.

*A **kanga** also called 'Leso' in Kenya was a rectangular shaped, 100% cotton, printed cloth with a brightly coloured decorative boarder around the outside that included a Bhanda proverb. Kangas were very popular*

77 The days of thunder

78 Kill him, kill him beast he stands at the gate of a kingdom that will be ours.

135

gifts especially for birthdays and weddings. Guests were presented with their own kangas, which was a sign of friendship. The kanga was also named "*ndege wa Guinea*" after the Swahili word for the spotted black and white guinea fowl. This is was due to the fact that the first *kangas* to be made used a similar print to that found on the guinea fowl, which was very classy and popular at the time.

Kangas were incredibly versatile although often worn as traditional African clothing. They were the ancient Bhanda royal and common gown, pyjama, casual and formal wear all in one. They were also worn by the bride, at Bhanda weddings and they were called '*kisutu*' in Swahili and their colours varied from white, black and red. Today, there are a large number of different *Kanga* designs available to purchase in the markets of Africa.

Kanga Bhanda Proverbs: *Usinisumbue* (don't bother me), *Adui mpende* (love your enemy), *Akili ni mali* (wits are wealth), *Mtaka yote hukosa yote* (one who wants all, usually loses all), *Kulekeza si kufuma* (to aim is not to hit), *Sina siri nina jibu* (I have no secrets but I have an answer).

When the gaur charged at Nazaar for the second time he evaded it again much to the dismay of the Egyptians but applause and roar of Bhanda people. It was like they were all watching a miracle manifesting itself upon everyone's sight and for the first time ever, Pharoah Narmer was both alarmed and intrigued by an opponent. He had heard tales about Nazaar but the stories were just mediocre compared to the legend himself! As the gaur kept coming and coming at Nazaar, the Bhanda king kept evading it until it got tired and fell down exhausted. Nazaar then went to it whilst it laid down unable to move and spoke softly whilst patting its neck gently but loud enough for everyone to hear.

Nazaar: *Oorwinning oor 'n viand is 'n strelende gevoel, maar*
            'n ongeregverdigde nederlaag, want dit is beter om te
            vergeet hoe dit alles begin het as om jouself te vergewe
            vir die wraak wat jy in woede geadministreer het,
            want dit bly by jou vir ewig![79]

            I aghaala otutu mmadu, anu ohia na chi obuladi
            mana udi gi di iche. Red na-ewe gi iwe di ka okwu
            iwe na-ewe m iwe! Anyi ghotara onwe anyi na gi.
            Ndi new anyi n'acho ime anyi ndi oru ma chusa anyi
            n'etiti onwe ha. [80]

            Asi havazive here kuti kana ukabata mukadzi
            wabata dombo? Abakwazi na ukuba wathinta
            umfazi wathinta imbokodo? [81]

Nazaar: You are tired now my cow friend, at the mercy of
            a man they sent you out to obliterate from this
            earth but look at them now gazing at you in dis-
            gust of the beast that you truly are! Power rules

79 Victory over a foe is a soothing feeling but an unwarranted defeat because
it is better to forget how it began than to forgive yourself for the vengeance you
administered in anger for that stays with you forever!

80 I have fought many people, beasts and gods even but your kind is different. Red infuriates you as lies enrage me! We understand each other you and
I. Your masters seek to make us slaves and scatter our women amongst themselves.

81 Don't they know that if you touch a woman you have touched a rock?

137

over them and the promise of coin even more so! But these are the masters who took you from the kingdom you knew to be served in a platter of juicy and delicious beef in mine! I have a message for my brother Theodore in the afterlife, please tell him that behold the first shall be last but the time is nigh and all is done!

With these last words Nazaar tied his red velvet kanga around the neck of the gaur and went to the nearest Egyptian soldier who stood mortified at what was happening, and unsheathed his sword, then he beheaded the gaur and left its dismembered body spewing blood all over. Nazaar looked straight at Narmer, and they both nodded as a sign of respect and recognition of each other's greatness as they glared at each other, as if they were speaking without other people noticing them.

Nazaar strode back in slow motion to the capital, taking in the praises and applaud that was coming from both camps for the first time in history. This was the first-time in war that even enemy soldiers hailed publicly the greatness of their foe but Nazaar was that type of a king who oozed and earned respect wherever he went or it was because he was literally born to do wonders! As he made it to the gate still taking in the praises, he quickly side stepped and evaded a spear that was meant to pin him to the gate. The spear was thrown from the Egyptians behind him but King Nazaar knew very well who had threw it.

The power and force it came at him with, could only be unleashed by a pure breed warrior, one that wielded the same blood as him, his brother, the traitor, Kane! However, Nazaar didn't even turn back to see who had thrown the spear and why it had been thrown, he just smiled and broke it into two and went inside. Kane seeing that his brother had passed his own personal test that he had set, grinned in both envy and disgust. Pharaoh Narmer smirked also but warned young Kane to avoid Nazaar in battle at all cost, because no matter how good of a fighter he was at the time, his bigger brother would beat him in battle!

So both camps resigned to a day of rest that day and the place where all this had taken place and the gaur was killed was called "kurwa nenzombe" by Narmer because he had seen the unimaginable survive the unthinkable! This marked the culture and sport of bull fighting even up to date! Human beings marvel at the entertainment and fun despite its complexities that have been culturally, traditionally and basically redefined throughout the ages!

Before the battle began, the Bhanda had all followed and kept their war rituals uniformly up to this particular date, therefore there was no time to waste any longer. The rituals included wearing a special garment and taking good care of the hair until it grew long, braiding it and decorating it with ochre and sheep fat. All Bhanda warriors drank no alcoholic beverages and ate only in the company of their age set. Sexual relations were prohibited until after the war. Throughout the war, until victory was accomplished or defeat had befell them, a Bhanda warrior served his people and king with honour. No one ran away as it was considered a taboo and to anger the gods to an extent that it made them punish the cowards with eternal fire upon death.

When the war finally broke out, the cavalry force of the Egyptians was large as Pharaoh Narmer fielded as many as 200,000 armed horsemen at the battle of *Mantengwane*. These horsemen were specialists with sabres and attacks with javelins, swords and bows. Nazaar on the other hand, organized his army to maximize the usage of handheld weapons in combination with tactical support from archers. Highly skilled hand-to-hand combat soldiers relied on their ability to dodge weapons rather than utilize the long shields they had and this was a big disadvantage to the Bhanda people.

However on largely suitable terrain such as that of the *Mantengwane*, the fast-moving Egyptian horsemen were the dominant force. When Nazaar saw this, he instructed *Changamire* to pull the Bhanda army from the level ground, forcing the Egyptians to fight on ground less favourable to their cavalry and this meant that the Egyptian horsemen were not as effective. The Bhanda began to turn the tide on them. Nazaar knew that if he had a fighting chance against the Egyptians, he had to fight them in segments.

Firstly, outside the capital, then finally, he would lure them inside the Bhanda capital where there were booby-traps all over the place. On the outfield battle outside, the Bhanda had to compress and mass compactly enough to stand against the Egyptian cavalry charges, of which the Bhanda could only do for a short while, due to the number and might of the Egyptian forces.

This was however all part of Nazaar's grand plan because when the battle got to a point when it seemed that the Egyptians were just a few minutes away from victory, the remaining Bhanda warriors that were holding the line on the battlefield would retreat and run back to the capital, leading to the Egyptians chasing after them. When the Egyptians chased them, phase two of the grand plan would be set in motion.

Booby traps and defensive works were an important part of warfare for the Bhanda Empire. The Palawa Bhanda tribe had created a unique type of field fortification, with trenches and low earthen embankments. These fortifications generally held up and against the Egyptians they changed the scope of the war in a significant way. When the Egyptians horsemen came racing and rushing to finish off the Bhanda, the only sound that was heard was all wailing men and horses as they both broke their bones on the trenches and spikes on the booby traps.

It was the kind of sound that Nazaar could get addicted to listening daily if it meant trampling all over his enemies like this! One by one the Egyptians began to fall in alarming numbers. The capital walls of the Bhanda capital were the world's longest man-made structure, and the series of earthen ramparts were the most extensive earthwork in the world. *Mantengwane* was situated in a geographical location that improved defensive and counter-attacking potential on a hill that had ridges, and it was protected by a double wall of trenches and ramparts.

Moreover the pathways along and around the capital concealed gullies and rows of sharp stones which hindered the Egyptian horses from moving and functioning as intended. Inner defences were laid out to dampen a successful breach with a maze of defensive walls allowing for entrapment and crossfire on enemy forces. In short, the Bhanda were gaining momentum and were killing and picking the Egyptians left, right and center due to the traps and fortifications all over the capital!

On the other side, supreme command for all forces rested with Pharaoh Narmer, but the two army groupings were under Prince Maahes and Prince Hor-Aha. In the Egyptian army, men of noble birth dominated the mounted units, and commoners were relegated to auxiliary foot formations, very similar to medieval European knights and foot soldiers. The main striking power of the Egyptian forces rested in the cavalry. The cavalry force, the (Golgota krag) was led by Prince Hor-Aha and it supervised the infantry, under Prince Maahes which consisted of Egyptian footmen slaves from conquered diverse tribes, who had predominately mastered the Egyptian art of war.

Both Nazaar and Narmer believed that archers had to generally open the battle, softening up the enemy for cavalry charges or the advance of the infantry. Egyptian soldiers tipped their swords and lances with poison before battle and the sling, a weapon more accurate than the early simple bow, destroyed the Bhanda Empire. Projectiles from a sling were so deadly especially the telluric iron made shot-put like balls/missiles used were the size of fists. The bow and sling were the weapons of choice for long distance warfare for the Bhanda Empire but the Egyptians came with a mace, and the heavy weapon was the first tool designed exclusively for war in Africa.

Narmer knew that the Bhanda would be cunning, resistant and would definitely give the Egyptians a good fight but the defensive walls of the capital and traps had caught him off-guard. Kane couldn't have known about them either since he was an outcast all his life and had never been to the big city! To counter-attack this sudden turn of events, the great Pharaoh instructed all his troops including the reserve unit that had all most the number of soldiers as the main unit to surround the capital. His plan was simple, if the Bhanda had traps all over the place and the Egyptians couldn't finish them off or draw them out, then they had to burn!

The Egyptians took they bows and tipped the arrows on oil before setting them alight on the bonfires they had set around the Capital gates. When the storm and hail of fire was let loose, the blues sky was over cast with a huge mist of Egyptian arrows as they killed and set alight everything they touched, pierced and fell on inside the Capital. One by one, children, mothers, fathers and the very absolute race of the Bhanda people was faced with the probability of extinction. Death was certain now because if the arrow didn't get you then the fire would. Houses burned and the royal house was the first to fall into ashes. There was no distinguishing between great warriors or a cowards, as there simple was no place to run or hide except to thesouth.

Ezansi was a secret escape gate that was south of the capital, and it was meant to be a fast exit route for the royal family if ever the Empire was under attack. However this wasn't the time for privilege and social statuses, the Empire faced extinction if its leaders didn't take immediate responses and sacrifices. So Nazaar made the only play and option that he had to save his people and buy them time to escape, he told his tribesmen and commanders to run! These were not the words of a king or better yet a renowned Bhanda warrior like Nazaar and so the people stood there puzzled at him stubbornly refusing to go because they feared the wrath of the gods, as they would be rendered cowards in the afterlife.

As the arrows kept raining on them, Nazaar rose in the mist of the smoke of the burning capital and stood at a rock that had been the general meeting point for *idale* (court) and addressed the few Bhanda people that were still alive! Around this rock, the Bhanda were safe because the arrows couldn't penetrate through the large wall that was behind it but the place could only accommodate a few of them. The others burned or were picked off by the Egyptian arrows as they tried to squeeze in too! Nazaar removed his crown and wept as he listened to the sounds of his people as they burned and gave up the ghost! He then broke the crown into four pieces and called Changamire, Xhii, Laibon Mbatian and Ndilimani to pick a piece each!

| King Nazaar: | Be of good cheer my brothers and sisters! Today we embrace a new feeling that we have never known, defeat! But be of good cheer my people for as the fire rises to destroy, it also rises to set apart a new era of greatness! My house has served |

you well and stood the test of time for centuries because of your obedience, submission and choice to live and be guided in the Bhanda ways of life by our rule, for that my family, I thank you everyone. *Ngiyabonga Bhanda osengoka zelusile*[82]."

I broke the crown into four pieces because we have always wanted to spread north, east, west and south and now we can! Rise Bhanda rise, show them wherever you go that we were not the fallen but those that found a new purpose and leap in life. Many if not all of you question my decision and ways today but I promise that you will understand why I did what I did someday, and when you do, rejoice, for my purpose is complete and my path is clear!

There was a man they called "**umpristi lomprofethi ezizweni**[83] and his name was Samuel. *Lindoda ithe isizayakubokhokho bayo eleziweni lamakhosi yathi,"kukhona na, engimkolodayo kumbe engimoneleyo? Uzulu waphendula wathi hayi!* (When this man was about to die and go to the afterlife, he asked the people if he owed anyone or if he had done ill to anyone and the multitude said no!). So I ask you today, this very moment, at the edge of

---

82 Thank you Bhanda, who now stands alone.

83 Priest or prophet of the nations

	our very fight for survival and brink of existence, do I owe you or have I done wrong to you, Bhanda?
Bhanda Empire:	*Che, ha u re kolote ebile ha ua re fosetsa.*[84]
King Nazaar	Then take heed and listen to me one last time brothers and sisters! For today you will scatter abroad to the ends of the world, in search of a land that you will call home but you shall fail for a time because a new era of civilization and modernization is upon us, and we are the last of the dying breed of true African patriarchs! Our culture is the only thing that will preserve and conserve us! Never lose sight of who you are and remember *"indoda iwa lamhlanje kusasa iphinde ivuke.*[85]
Changamire:	I took a vow to follow you to the death *Mnyamana*, and today you want us to condemn ourselves and children to" to hell? I refuse to live you to die alone at the hands of these northern men!
King Nazaar:	I admire you brother! You are a Bhanda to the core but it is not your time yet and these people will need a leader to guide them through the wilderness and plains for the dark days are coming,

84 No you don't owe us nor have you wronged us Great one

85 A man falls today and rises tomorrow!

where brother shall devour brother for coin and amusement of the foreigners! Be strong *"Dombo lama Dombo, bathembe wena mfowethu! Nyamezela, kuzolunga qhawe lamaqhawe!* Now go before it is too late... Go!* [86]

Xhii: *Bayethe Nkosi! Bayethe Ngangozulu! Bayethe...* [87]

As the people set course making a run for their lives out of the capital being led by Changamire and the other three generals, it was crystal clear that hearts were heavy and tears were threatening to flow. For Changamire on the other hand, this was a blessing and curse because not only did he have to take over the remnants of a fallen empire, he had to survive attacks from other smaller tribes, whilst conserving the little that they still had.

Nazaar knew very well that his brother in-law was capable of that duty but what shocked everyone was *Nondindwa's* decision to stay behind with her brother! She chose death with alongside her brother other than to rulre with her husband! This act was called *ukuhlamuka lokuthatheka* [88] in Bhanda culture, Nondindwa had one sole purpose in life and that was to live and abide by her husband's side forever! Her choice to serve and be in the company of another man, whether it was her brother or not, served to make her underrated and a cultural embar-

---

86 Be strong Changamire Dombo, they are dependent on you now brother, be patient and steadfast great warrior!

87 Hail the king, hail the greatest, hail.

88 To betray and to be easily carried away

rassment, moreover it made her a princess who lacked morals! Nazaar neither judged her actions nor spoke ill of her choice because he knew that it was too late for both either way but Changamire cursed her, when he realised what had happened. This has followed many women who betray their man for another, and there are called "*oNondindwa*[89]" due to Changamire's curese.

As the Bhanda people fled, a small group of boys and girls called *iyasa*[90], dancers and singers by trade, deserted the group and decided to curse and face the Egyptians head on. Their strategy was simple, sing and dance until the gods themselves rose up to avenge the spilt Bhanda blood and fallen heroes. As they deserted the group being led by their most gifted performer, Toekomstige the Egyptians mounted on horsebacks, chariots with spikes and armed with strong iron swords as well as civilized and modern battlefield tactics, wiped them out before they could even play their "*mbira and marimba.*"

Today a clinch stands unsolved as a group called "*Iyasa*" was formed in 2001 in Bulawayo, and its lead member was called Future meaning "toekomstige" in Afrikaans! Nonetheless, the *iyasa* managed to drag the attention of the Egyptians for a while whilst Nazaar and Nondindwa were making their way out of the cloud of smoke and rubble of the burned capital. As they got close to what was left of the walls and gate, Nondidwa asked her brother the question that was lingering on her mind!

89 A lady that is easily carried away and has loose morals
90 Freedom of youth

Nondindwa:	Who told you about the priest and prophet or whatever that is?
King Nazaar:	Sierra the Egyptian! He is my friend, he told me a longtime ago after I captured him and 4 other Egyptians!
Nondindwa:	So we are truly defeated then? First they tell you their stories, break bread with us and now they burn and flag us with weapons as fleas and ticks at the back of a healthy mule! How ironic that we are what's left of the royal family excluding that *thing* that sold us out to the Egyptians!
King Nazaar:	That "thing" is the only reason why I am still alive because it should have never seen the light of day and I intend to take it with me to the afterlife as a gift to the Bhanda gods!
Nondindwa:	What if you fail brother? What if that *thing* is directly from the gods and wasn't meant to die?
King Nazaar:	Then rest assured that the world as people know it will change, for power consumes even the timid and kind at heart. At times and for the born and raised in evil, the world would be in total chaos!
Nondindwa:	So did you do it then brother? Kill all your wives and children?

King Nazaar: Custom demands that I do in verge of defeat and
                  so I did without mercy because as much as that
                  killed me spiritually and physically, I will rest at
                  ease knowing that my family didn't suffer a pain-
                  ful death, my wives wherein made Egyptian har-
                  lots and my children slaves! You are blessed today
                  sister because you embrace a death that is truly
                  certain and for that, I am sure you will rule as
                  queen in the afterlife!

Nondindwa: *Anyi bu nwanne anyi!*[91]

As Nazaar and Nondindwa came out of the clouds of smoke into
plain sight, for every Egyptian to see, Narmer was both thrilled and impressed! In all his life he ruled and conquered by the sword effortlessly
but never had he seen someone who did the same even in defeat! The
Egyptian soldiers made way for them, mocking and spitting on them
as they walked towards the man of the moment. The victorious and
undisputed Narmer who however ordered every soldier that had done
this to cut off their middle finger!

This was punishment for disgracing a man and opponent that
Narmer himself saw as more than a king! In another lifetime, Narmer
wished that Nazaar was born an Egyptian and his brother, because
he felt that they had a mutual understanding and take on life but unfortunately things had come to the very end, and such is everything
that comes to life! Narmer finally spoke to Nazaar Bottom of Format

---

91 We are who we are brother!

Namoratunga, an archaeological site on the west side of Lake Turkana in present day Kenya. Namoratunga meant "people of stone" in the Bhanda Turkana language, and it contained 19 basalt pillars, which were surrounded by a circular formation of stones.

It was the burial sight of all Bhanda kings which was sometimes called the *Lokori*. Namoratunga was also a place of divine mysticism where traditional royalists and leaders tied constellations or stars to the 12-month, 354-day lunar calendar of the Bhanda people. In short, this was also where they read the stars, and where royal sheepherders used to go to dance and sing lullabies to the fallen Bhanda kings.

Pharoah Narmer: Shall we began?

King Nazaar: A penny for your thoughts before we commence this unfortunate debacle dear *friend*! You stand in sacred ground today, dishonouring the memory of all Bhanda kings and queens but who am I to speak of might when I have suffered death today? I only ask for one favour, spare the little of what remains of my brethren and do not go after them!

Pharoah Narmer: What seal shall bind this accord between us dear *friend* for even if I kill them or not, it still does matter to me because we both understand the spoils and implications of war?

King Nazaar: The Princess shall be the seal and a covenant of understanding between us. Her hand in marriage will seal this accord and our people will be spared because of this understanding!

Pharaoh Narmer: So let it be *"brother!"*

After all was agreed, Narmer and Nazaar both went inside the arc of the Namoratunga and were surrounded by the Egyptian soldiers and their new queen! Nazaar and Nondindwa both knew that the sacrifice they had made that day, would shape the whole course of their people lives' and Africa as a whole but it had to be done to save a race! When the fight between Narmer and Pharoah began, both men had removed their armour but Nazaar refused to carry a weapon alluding to the fact that he was skilled enough to take Narmer's sword from him and kill him with it at will!

Everybody laughed at this assertion except Kane, Nondindwa and Narmer himself because whilst the Egyptian soldiers were misguided by their own Pharoah's combat skills, Nondindwa, Kane and Narmer knew very well how good Nazaar was. Nazaar had never lost a fight, not because he was lucky or cheated but because he was the perfection of a war machine. He understand how his enemy breathed when they were afraid, and how they reacted when they thought they had the upper hand, and when they were about to swing a weapon or make a block. He saw their pressure points and weak spots, before they even began the fight. One swing after the other, Nazaar evaded all of them until Pharoah Narmer got tired and by this time there was dead silence! Everyone finally understood why *UMnyamana* was the undisputed Champion, not only of the Bhanda Empire but Africa itself!

Nazaar then fulfilled his promise and out-maneuvered the Pharaoh and took his sword from him to the worry and discomfort of all the Egyptians! They had never seen a man outclass Narmer in combat before and what made it worse was that it was so effortless that someone would think it was just a sparring session between master and student. To their reality, this was the undisputed Egyptian Pharaoh and warrior being schooled in the art of war, by a man born to deliver nothing more than the best fight!

As Narmer stood at the mercy of Nazaar, Nazaar did the unthinkable, a trick that gave Narmer his sword back but at the same time stabbing Nazaar deeply in the chest! Narmer stood shocked and almost shaking, his soldiers however were convinced that their Pharoah had finally out-witted Nazaar and made the definitive move and cheered him loudly! Nazaar bleeding heavily and seeing that Narmer was losing the script as he was still shaking, fell on his knees and whispered to him!

King Nazaar: Do it! Its time brother and its better this way!

Narmer was shaking and still in disbelief of what had just happened. Kane was the only one who had seen what happened, therefore he came quick and fast and stabbed Nazaar from the back with a spear, much to the applause and cheer of the crowd! As Nazaar was about to die he cursed Kane because he was a coward that couldn't face him man to man but opted to back-stab him!

King Nazaar: Know this, young brother, you have killed me today and won their hearts for a day but tomorrow comes with a price and these people will never accept you as one of them! You shall rule and get the power that you thirst so much for but it shall kill you someday as it has me! For a storm comes in the days to come when the fallen shall be strong and undivided again.... I pity you when that day comes brother, for you shall witness an excruciating death and pain that will shake every bone and threshold of your soul!

Nazaar the great *Mnyamana*, finally died and Narmer buried him himself with Nondindwa his wife. He was laid next to Menelick his father, and other fallen Bhanda kings and his tomb was unique, because it was the first pyramid tomb made for a king that wasn't in Egypt or an Egyptian! Narmer kept his promise and never went after the Bhanda people and Kane finally got his wish and became the new king of the new Egyptian lands that were previously Bhanda territory! Nondindwa and all the women of Egypt including Queen Neithhotep, Narmer's first wife met at the Namoratunga site in December every year, to seek divine intervention for issues affecting their lives and largely to honour the Bhanda kings especially Nazaar, because he had spared the life of their king in order for his own people to live.

Chapter 5
(The Beginning
And End)

The destruction of the Bhanda Empire was a sudden and catastrophic fiasco with a fixed and inevitable impetus, on the shape and map of Africa, as it was leading to the scramble of Africa before the West even dreamt of it! Changamire tried to hold the tribes together as they journeyed all over Africa, conquering other smaller and weaker kingdoms and tribes. However, as Nazaar had predicted, they hadn't found a place to call home yet, and wherever they went they were welcomed with great hostility.

Despite of everything, the Bhanda tribe did not split because of succession issues or gold or greed, it split because of salt! Salt from the Sahara desert was one of the major *trade* goods of ancient **Africa,** where very little, naturally occurring deposits of the mineral could be found. It was transported via camel caravans, and by boat along such rivers as the Niger and Senegal. Salt found its way to trading centers like Koumbi Saleh, Niani, and Timbuktu, where it was passed further south or exchanged for other goods such as ivory, hides, copper, iron, and cereals. The most common exchange was salt for gold dust and this led to the first Scramble of Africa!

Salt was always in great demand in order to better preserve dried meat and to give added taste to food, particularly with the beginning of the intense and ever improving agricultural mode of life in Africa. Hunters and food-gatherers such as the Hadza and San Bhanda tribes obtained a large amount of their salt intake from the animals they had hunted, and from fresh plant food. When the salt mineral deposits were found by the Akhan tribe in salt mines of Idjil, Awlil and Taghaza in the Sahel, every tribe wanted to lay claim to this new found commodity and power! Every king knew that whoever controlled the salt trade also controlled the gold trade, and both were the principal economic pillars of all African empires at the time.

Changamire, seeing the opportunity for power, supremacy and resurrection again of the Bhanda might, attempted to muscle in on the salt market. He arranged for several prominent African salt trader tribe leaders such as uNdogu and Soke of the Dizra and Ciloshe tribes respectively to be murdered at Taghaza. However the Bhanda suffered another crushing defeat as Changamire's plan failed dismally when Mansa Musa Keita 1, came to the aid of the targeted tribes that faced the danger of being stomped by the Bhanda juggernaut!

Musa Keita I was an extremely powerful leader, and under his leadership Manden Kurufaba had conquered 24 cities in the medieval East and Western Africa. He had a great deal of nick names and titles, including the *'Lion of Manden Kurufaba'* and *'Conqueror of Ghanata'*. Under his rule, *Manden Kurufaba* was one of the wealthiest Empires in the world due to the gold and salt production and trade, agriculture and imperialism.

He was the richest man to ever live in this world even up to date with a net worth of 400billion US dollars. One of his nicknames, *'Lord of the Mines of Wangara,'* was due to the fact he was in control of all the gold and salt mines there. Thus contributing to his wealth which other tribes and kingdoms described as "mind-bogglingly wealth." Wealth meant power and the ability to command and hire a large unit of mercenaries and soldiers and fortunately enough, Mansa Musa had both! On his squabble with Changamire for the control of salt and gold mines, he crushed what was left of the Bhanda resistance and forces in a matter of minutes! It was both a swift and humiliating defeat but even worse, the final toll on the defragmented and dying Bhanda Empire!

Musa Kieta I, was famed for his legendary pilgrimage to Mecca with over 60,000 attendants, 12,000 slaves and lavish outpouring of gold to the poor across Sahel region, Egypt and the Middle East, which meant that he had the capacity to build mosques each and every Friday as long as he lived. In the entire human history, this was the only time that one man directly controlled the price of gold and salt in the Mediterranean. His wealth, ambition and foreign policy drew the initial attention and attraction of Europeans to Africa, and even worse the undisputed Pharaoh Narmer and his new alien and puppet king, Kane the to a direct collision with him.

Mansa Musa was in charge of vast land. He ruled all (or parts) of modern day Mauritania, Senegal, Gambia, Guinea, Burkina Faso, Manden Kurufaba, Niger, Nigeria, and Chad. So when the Egyptian and the Manden Kurufaba forces clashed in Timbuktu, it wasn't just a regular war, it was world war one in the African continent! It didn't matter if a particular tribe wasn't involved but the impact and side effects of that war were experienced all over Africa. This shaped the new era of trade, agriculture and livelihoods in Africa as tribes tried to cope with the after effects of the war and the sudden shocks!

The Timbuktu War

As the Bhanda tribe dispersed and broke into four with each segment caring a piece of king Nazaar's crown, the general feeling was that the Empire was over. Therefore it was now time to go separately and seek new lands and docile territory to inhabit and mend their bruised and totally decimated egos! Another reason for the split was that Nazaar had instructed them to go in all directions and seek a land to call home, thus to cover more ground, the Bhanda tribes had to break into segments that covered North, East, West and South in their pursuit of a new home.

Kane/Maahes "the king of Africa"

When Kane took over Egypt, in 17 military campaigns, he had 17 victories and this was the birth of the imperialist period of the greatest civilization of all time. He was an invincible Pharaoh that was obsessed with his mark in eternity and rose to the absolute summit of the history of the black world. Kane had learnt from the weakness of the Bhanda tribe and his first initiative was security enhancement which actually gave birth to absolute Egyptian imperialist policy. However a powerful neighboring tribe called the Mitanni, that resided in present-day Iraq challenged the power of Egypt.

At the battle of Meggido, a fortified city were the Mitannians and their coalition were residing, Kane used a powerful network of secret services called "inhloli" to learn about his enemy's coalition that was stationed at the fortified city of Megiddo. Despite the contrary opinion of his generals and the fatigue of his troops, he decided to go through the difficult terrain of Aruna to surprise his opponents. The Egyptians surrounded the city from its mountainous heights and inflicted relentless attacks on it. They dug giant pits around it and besiege it for 7 months.

Megiddo was finally crushed by the Egyptian blockade and assaults as the Mitannian coalition was weakened by hunger also therefore leading to inevitable surrender and this victory led to Kane being revered and loved as the new and absolute "Father of United Egypt". One by one all the tribes fell and submitted to the great Pharaoh in North Africa. The Bedouins, ancestors of the Arabs, were also defeated by Kane, who extended his control over Arabia and stretched the reach and glory of the Egyptian Empire to its furthest influence and height ever. All the kings of the conquered regions hastened to give their daughters to the "king of Africa" as some began to call him as a sign of allegiance. One of the tribes that was in danger of succumbing to the Egyptian imperialist swagger was Sheba because of their queen and their belief.

Kane believed that he wasn't chosen by the gods or supernatural elite to rule, he believed that he was the god of the gods and goddesses just like Zeus was to the Greeks hence he called himself Amun-Ra meaning the invisible god of the sun, order, kings, queens, the sky and underworld. Any other religion besides his belief was null and void and ultimately deserved to be wiped out totally! The Queen of Sheba was a threat to his belief because of her faith in Christianity and because out of all the queens that Kane had been offered as wives, she was the only one who had rejected his courtship! For a man who took what he wanted and violated what he didn't, this rejection led to the common weak and evil act and idiom of *"If I can't have you then no one will,"* as Kane declared war on Sheba.

The Queen of Sheba

Many have encountered the phrase *"who does she think she is - the Queen of Sheba?"* at some point but don't know about the real Queen of Sheba, and what she did of noteworthy to coin the phrase. **Makeda the Queen of Sheba** was a queen of incredible strength. She had survived gruesome and countless battles such the one against the serpent king Awre. The serpent king had been troubling the northern Ethiopian kingdom of Axum and after defeating the serpent king, Makeda became the queen of Axum.

Makeda was famous for her story with the biblical figure, King Solomon of Jerusalem. They had a son named Menelik I (or Ebna la-Hakim), meaning "son of the wise." Their son became the first imperial ruler of Ethiopia and the first of a line of Aksûmite kings. And according to legend, Makeda and her son brought back the biblical Ark of the Covenant to Axum and through them, the lineage of great East African and Nubian kings was born. The remains of a grand stone palace in Aksum, which is in present day Ethiopia, is where the home of the Queen of Sheba was, and she left a legacy as an essential figure in Old Testament history for the Ethiopian Orthodox Church.

This was the queen that Kane wanted to both kill and humiliate for refusing his proposal to be his queen and submit to the his religion and Kane thought this was going to be easy. He looked at how Egypt dwarfed Sheba in every way militarily, economically and holistically and laughed at his enemies' inevitable demise before the war even began! However, Kane made one miscalculation and that mistake defined his reign forever.

Kane forgot that during the civil war and power conflicts of succession in Egypt, other tribes had been growing both economically and militarily and Sheba under their great Queen were part of those kingdoms that were breaking new ground! Queen Makeda knew that men like Kane understood one language and that was "force." There was no reasoning or truce with evil and barbaric men such as Maahes in her sight and spiritually, he was the "devil's advocate" literally in her sight and to cast out such a principality of darkness, the queen had to seek help.

She could pray if she desired too and left it to Yahweh to assist her but she understood that God helps those who help themselves and take the first initiative towards His will and glory therefore she had to seek the strongest alliance ever if she was to stand a chance against Kane! Faced with such burden and cries from his scared people, the Queen of Sheba firstly sought the assistance of Christian kings and queens, in the hope of not only winning the war as well but to also spread Christianity in all borders as well.

Ezana Axum was the first Ethiopian king and ally that joined the Queen of Sheba's *Seleka* since Ethiopia was a very large area that was inhabited by many independent kings and queens at the time. Ezana Axum was also the first Ethiopian King to embrace Christianity and convert his entire kingdom. He was a kind ruler and he cared deeply about the happiness of his people and he was a monument builder, erecting a number of obelisks. In war he fought with religious fervour that made some of his opponents conform to Christianity and conversion before they were wiped away. His armies had highly skilled archers who had a tactical advantage over their sword-wielding, horse-mounted enemies.

The second Christian King to join the Queen of Sheba's Seleka was **King Mvemba Nzinga** ruler of the Kongo Empire. Mvemba Nzinga was a powerful king who changed the religious paradigm of the Bakongo people (the founders of the Kongo Empire). Mvemba's father, Nzinga Nkuwu, had been the first Kongo king to become a Christian but on his death bed, he denounced Christianity as he was also dedicated to his traditional beliefs. King Mvemba Nzinga wrested power from his brother upon his father's death in a brief civil war and became king.

On his ascension to the throne, he ordered the religious structure of Kongo to change to accommodate his new faith. This was huge in Kongo because he literally became bigger than tradition itself. The change took power away from traditional advisors, priest/shamans and even the *"ne mbanda-mbanda*[92]*"* shifting power in a new direction, one that he controlled with much authority. King Mvemba built many churches and schools, boosting literacy and education largely for the *Manikongo*.[93] His son Dom Henrique was the Bishop of Utica in what is now Tunisia. He was an avid seeker of knowledge and even educated himself in foreign laws in order to take what he could use for his people.

However, some Christian kings refused to assist the Queen of Sheba because of fear and the price that awaited anyone who had allied with her, in the event that the undisputed and mighty Egyptian Empire prevailed again. Therefore Makeda had to change strategy and ally with the fearless and strongest in the continent even if they had differences

92 The royal council
93 Kongo elites

in belief and culture for the sake of all Africa and no one was fearless and strong as *Oba Ewuare "the Great," Behanzin Hossu Bowelle "the King Shark"* and *Ntu*. These men were not ordinary kings, they were men that understood what it meant to go into war with a big bully like Kane and stand victorious after they had spanked and taught him some manners!

The Queen of Sheba needed them all if she was to save herself and her people from Kane's merciless grasp but out of all the allies, she needed **Ntu** the most regardless of his beliefs as an African traditionalist! You see Ntu was born out of the burning flames of the fallen Bhanda Empire and was an orphan since birth due to the events that transpired at the time. When he grew up under the regiments of Changamire Dombo, he trained and swore to avenge his parents and take back his people's lands from the enemy and his nemesis, Kane himself! Kane was the one who had killed his father and ordered his men to rape his mother to death! Therefore Ntu grew up with a score to settle and the time for vengeance had arrived!

Ntu the father of the "AbaNtu"

King 'Ntu, became the ancestor of all African people that went to the south after the destruction of the Bhanda Empire and the fall of all idolised leaders such as Xhii with time. The plural noun 'abantu' was a result of Ntu's name being used in plural form to categorize his descendants. Ntu was a descendant of Yeye of Godongwana, descendant of Hhamu/**Ham** of **Ishmael** otherwise known as **Abraham** who had fathered him to his slave Hagayi/**Hagar**. After Changamire's death, what was left of the Bhanda people in the South of Africa was a torn

162

remnant of an old wild bull that had seen better days!

Changamire had tried his best to save his people and find a peaceful and receptive land that they could inhabit and rebuild their empire in again but time and unamendable 'scars' were just too much for the kingdom that he now called the Rozwi Empire. Ntu rose up in this time of great turmoil and was chosen as the new leader after Changamire's death. When the Queen of Sheba arrived with the plea of a coalition against his arch nemesis, Ntu agreed immediately before the Queen had even finished speaking and the clinche was that Ntu was born from a religious background of both Christianity and African traditional religion.

Although his father was a radical African traditionalist, therefore the Christian element in his family was phased out before he was even born. When the time for war against Kane was nigh, Ntu left his son Mnguni in power whilst he took a segment of his *"abahlaseli[94]"* army to war and it is through Mnguni that amaNguni and abeSuthu were born as he continued the search for a home for his fathers' people,*"abantu"* as they now called themselves.

On penetrating Southern Africa, *abeSuthu* divided into three groups i.e. *abeSuthu* of *Mshweshwe, amaPedi* and *amaTswana. AmaNguni* divided into five groups, i.e. *amaNguni, amaMbo, amaNtungwa Nguni, amaLala Nguni, amaDebe Nguni* and *amaThonga*. All these were the descendants of the sons of Mnguni the son of Ntu. A development of a new group of *amaSwazi* emerged from *amaMbo*. Under *amaNtungwa* a group of *amaZulu* emerged.

Under *amaDebe* then emerged *amaBhaca* while *amaThonga* re-

94 The attackers

mained a separate group. *AmaLala* then gave birth to the *Mthwethwa* kinship group. The *amaNtungwa Nguni* were led by Luzimane *kaMnguni*, Mnguni's son and they inhabited Babanango, Nkandla, Msinga lands. Meanwhile *amaMbo* and the other groups moved along the coast towards the Bombo, Swazini and Ngwavuma. Ntu's lineage can be summarized as follows: Ntu, Mnguni, Gumede, Qwabe, Mnguni Luzimane Malandela, Qwabe and Zulu. Zulu was the father of Senzangakhona who fathered Shaka Zulu the famous African Zulu king!

Oba Ewuare "the Great"

Oba Ewaure was the most celebrated King in all of Benin and a key member of the *seleka* that fought the evil and cunning king in Africa. Not only was he great because of his political changes but because of his pioneering spirit. He was one of the few kings in Africa who travelled widely all over Africa, as far as Guinea to the west and Congo in the south and this gave him incredible experience, training and most of all wisdom. Under his reign, Benin began a period of strong central government as he established an impressive State Council and State Bureaucracy.

He created the native doctor guilds assigning them titles, built many roads in Benin City and the greatest innermost wall to keep out invaders. Oba Ewaure exemplified the expression "master of all trades." He was a powerful and courageous leader whose armies moved through the forest defeating town after town and even created a tradition of stable succession, by starting a strategic policy which removed the conquered town's chieftains from absolute power but allowed them power in a congressional committee.

He conquered and absorbed at least 201 surrounding towns and villages during his reign and outside of war, Ewuare was a charismatic leader that established several cultural traditions, communal events and festivals. He was such a powerful man that many believed he held magical powers, which is attested too much of the artwork of his era. An annual festival called the *Igue* festival was held to renew his magical powers and it is still celebrated in Benin to this day.

Last but not least, **Béhanzin (Gbêhanzin) Hossu Bowelle aka the "King Shark"** was the final member of *"Dagaalyahanada xorriyadda*[95]*" seleka* as was eventually tagged! Unlike his other alliance members, Béhanzin (Gbêhanzin) Hossu Bowelle knew the Egyptians' capabilities and mind games very well as he had faced them before under Pharaoh Narmer.

Béhanzin (Gbêhanzin) Hossu Bowelle "The King Shark"

Béhanzin (Gbêhanzin) Hossu Bowelle, which translates to "the egg of the world" or the son of the shark" was known colloquially as 'The King Shark' and was arguably one of the most powerful rulers of Africa. He commanded a powerful army served by both 150,000 male and 5000 infamous Amazon women and was a courageous and wise ruler to his people. However, Egypt under the late Pharaoh Narmer had once attempted to take over his empire, in a feat to capitalize the atmosphere of a civil war that was within his kingdom where an ambitious sect of Egyptian bribed opposition, had risen to challenge and make him a victim of a great deal of propaganda and chaos.

Eventually, he overcame the opposition even when they had portrayed him as a vicious king, who ruled over savages that followed him

95   Meaning freedom fighters in Somalese.

blindly. The King Shark being famous for nodding his head whenever he meant life or death of his subjects, gave a mass nod to his executioner, to kill all those that had been bribed by the Egyptians. Using a "Ngulu/ ngolo/ ngwolo/ntsaka" sickle blade, this mass execution was called "*letsatsi la lere le kulang*[96]" and also marked the official enmity between Egypt and the King Shark. So when the Queen of Sheba came with the roll call for an alliance against a common enemy, it was a no brainer that the king Shark would join the gang.

In the early break of winter when the mist was all over and the dew, and frost bites were vexing the upper lands of the Sahara and Sahel plateaus, and inhabitants, the "Gusu" war began! It wasn't the conditions that made this war an epic battle of all time, it was simply the "belief" that people were serving and offering themselves, whether in victory or demise, for a higher cause than themselves, therefore no one had anything to lose!

It was a religious blood bath for whoever won and lost because winning meant   having sinned, for killing thousands of potential saints. However losing on the other hand meant that the sacrificed blood would be used to wash away the sins of the victor in their glorious bathtubs, and this was viewed as sacrilege in all types and forms of religion at the time! For having inaugurated the greatest imperialist period of the critical civilization of all time, Kane remains the greatest pharaoh of Egypt but one of the most evil African kings to have walked on Earth. Engraved on the walls of Karnak, Kane had a vibrant hymn of war written in which he guided Egypt from victory to victory until the "Gusu" war. It was a cataclysmic Armageddon that ended with country sized

96   The day of the sickle blade

ashes of ruptured skulls and lost souls, all for the price of freedom!

The Gusu War

Gusu was virgin land that was in between North, West, East and Southern Africa. It was believed to be enchanted territory and god land because no one dared cross it or even took a dump when they passed near it! For the Christian leaders such as the queen of Sheba this was one of the barbaric and trivial beliefs they wanted to eradicate through a modern and Christian approach to life! However, for African traditionalist such as Ntu, this was the land that they believed, kings died and were reborn in, even though there wasn't even one skeleton to signal the existence of any living specie, or myths they believed in!

Kane on the other hand wanted to be the sovereign ruler of both man and gods, therefore conquering his rivals in this divine and untainted land would seal his dream as the absolute ruler of everything below and above! Therefore the land was called *iGusu* to signify untouched, divine and sacred land that harboured many myths and hidden mysteries about the world itself, and the powers and principalities that shape it by force or will! Today *iGusu* is called Central Africa and is also a word and term used to define a clustered and bushy area! Only a few know that it was a prohibited to cross from the north to the south or west to the east or vice versa through central Africa, because it was believed that the gods destroyed everyone who dared to even pluck out a tree leaf out of the *Gusu* lands!

However the fight against Kane demanded men and women who could put aside their vast differences and beliefs, and tap in the can of this absurd human word called "limitations"! This was a war made to taste everybody's limits and only those without would make it alive. As the war was about to begin, a miracle happened, before the first kill had even been made. At the center of the grass fields where the cradle/foundation of *iGusu* was, a prominent rock shelter site in the Laka Valley near present day northwest Cameroun called **Shum Laka,** was found! A heap of varying bones and an underground citadel underneath was found as the battle field collapsed, due to the marching of the armies as they braced themselves for a full scale collision. This shook everyone including the great queens and kings themselves because from what they could see and tell, this city predated their very existence as African tribes, and therefore the general assumption was that this was the underground lair of gods, as some of the bones were too thick and big to be human bones.

Despite the tropical climate that wasn't ideal for bone preservation, the Shum Laka revealed surprising discoveries, especially of two giant skulls that had gold ornaments in their canines, and occipital back bone area of the skull! The belief was that, the skulls were of the old gods that had transformed and moved their divine essence and being from human form like-features to a more spiritual and omnipresent form of being, whilst the gold ornaments were just residue from the gold blood that ran through their godly bodies! Therefore the place was called Shum Laka to acknowledge the existence of an ancient ancestry of the Shum Laka gods and children from a previously unknown African lineage, distantly related to present-day Africans. Whether this was just a logical discovery or a surprise didn't matter but the underlining fact was that the world was much older and complex than the history that everybody knew. The biggest questions was what had happened to the children of Shum Laka? And were they wiped out and replaced by pres-

168

ent and more modern form of divine deity? Or where they just a typical ancient civilization?

Kane however was not overly amused by these sudden developments and discovery. To him, it didn't matter what race or god had been found or ruled the rubble in the underground, what mattered was that he was going to conquer and destroy anything that stood in his way, and for the first time ever, he and the Queen of Sheba agreed on something.,

This discovery was a danger in swaying the war to a sudden and abrupt war because of varying religious beliefs, as a large number of warriors and captains were shaken when the discovery was made. It was like they had found a new lease of life and some of them even knelt down to worship a god that they didn't even know existed before the Shum Laka came to light! Kane knew that he had to discredit this site with all means possible if war was to commence as intended and so did the Queen of Sheba since she as a Christian, didn't believe in pagan beliefs although the discovery was quite shocking and eye opening. So Kane decided to do one thing he knew very well would not only anger the Queen of Sheba's *seleka* to war but also swear everlasting hatred upon the Egyptians by peeing on the giant skulls as he sang a mocking song!

Pharaoh Maahes: *"Mapenzi anopfugamira vamwari vanonwa piss yangu uye zvakadaro ivo vanomira kuti varwe neni... kana vari mapenzi, ivo vachawa!"* (Fools kneel for gods that drink my piss and yet they stand to fight me... fools they are... and fools they shall fall!)

Queen of Sheba: When they hang your insides and celebrate by pluck your fingers, one by one, remember this very moment great king... for you have played the fool for assuming that you are a god when we serve a higher and sovereign Almighty God and King of kings! You have blasphemed against these men's gods and I dare not to stand in their way when they break the skull of your men and children, and raid your wives as you watch the fruits of your own mouth lay your Empire to waste!

Pharoah Maahes: A throne chaired by a woman is like an unborn baby that kicks the air that it doesn't see but an alliance that even stands the idea of breaking bread with one, is like a leper who only blinks and smiles when another skin lesion appears and thinks its puberty whilst they are rotting from the inside out! Do you know why my men are disallowed to touch women during the times of war my Queen? It's because women make men weak... a legend becomes a folklore and potential goes to waste after great men bed women! The history has been kind to men who have, and this is why we stay pure and keep on winning my Queen! I understand that you think that these men will assist you and maybe they will but how long do you think it will take for them to see that you tricked and led them to their death, as I slice open the bellies of their loved ones time and time again?

King Ntu: *Uyadelela lo! Ufuna usuthu!... usuthu ... usuthu!*
                       (He is undermining us, so let the war begin!)

"Usuthu!" cried the *Abantu* squadron, infuriated and armed with spears and long shields made of cowhide, as they charged, being led by Ntu at the Egyptians due to Kane's act of mocking the gods! Usuthu was a faction in Ntu's Kingdom, and they took their name from a type of cattle that their warrior ancestors used to pillage during wars. To keep alive their memory, and to summon the power of their brave forbearers, the *Abantu* would shout out *"Usuthu!"* during battle and this tradition was passed on until the eventual birth of the Zulu kingdom and Shaka himself who made it more famous than his predecessors!

King Shark: **"Allahu akbar... allahu akbar..!"**

"Allahu Akbar!" cried Béhanzin (Gbêhanzin) Hossu Bowelle "The King Shark" as his warriors also charged at the Egyptians from a different direction that mirrored the *Abantu's* charge! Takbir, the term used for the Muslim phase "Allahu Akbar!" *God is great!* Was used for a variety of settings including births, deaths, and celebrations, but ultimately it was the traditional battle cry. Most ancient Muslim rulers used the Takbir as a war cry in the battle and as years went by it was subsequently and eventually shouted by Muslim soldiers during crusades. Today, of course, the phrase has become infamous in the West for its use in terrorist attacks.

The first warrior to fall wasn't killed by the tip of a spear of the clash of the opposing legions, he was simple swept aside by force and speed that both opponents came crushing into each other by. It was like a loud thundering strike had hit the land when body crushed upon body, as some warriors lost composure and balance at the boiling place of the battle. Everyone could hear the *Abantu* as they killed without mercy whilst using the Roman cohort and shield system of defending enemy strikes and then counter-attacking them.

"Vula... Vala... Ngadla..!" These were the three words spoken by Ntu and stages of combat that his *Abantu* were masters of. **Vula** was the act of making way for all regiments from the back of the main force to come into the front when some of the warriors were tired to refresh and strengthen the main force. **Vala** was the second stage and this was the act of enclosing the enemy in a cow-horn formation such that they would be deflected to the killing zones of the attacker.

Ngadla was the final command and act, and this was straight forward as it sounds, kill! Mvemba Nzinga's Kongonians, Ezana Axums's Ethiopians and the Queen of Sheba's Shebanians fought with a Christian fervour that made some of the Egyptians to question their entire faith and beliefs. Before death and the eventually choke of blood as it choked the bleeding and fallen Egyptian warrior, all Kongonians, Shebanians and Ethiopians were drilled in the art of praying and wishing their defeated foe well even in death, by doing a cross like gesture and blowing a kiss to the sky! This was believed to be a sign of remorse and both glorifying the presence of God in the battle, and these armies had abundant and highly skilled archers who had a tactical advantage over their sword-wielding, horse-mounted Egyptians.

Oba Ewuare the Great's Beninians attacked the Egyptians from the rear as Dagaalyahanada xorriyadda *seleka* leaders had planned and agreed. As his warriors fought the Egyptians they used everything within the environment to their advantage. If there was a gully the Beninese would push the Egyptian regiments towards it until they fell and were easy and clear targets for the *seleka*! If there was dust, the Beninians used the wind to blow it towards the Egyptians so that they would be blinded for a short while whilst the Beninians advanced on them, and killed them easily. Everything was an advantage to the Beninians as their wise and intelligent leader had taught them. For every Egyptian that fell, the Beninese that had struck him/her dead had to do a small ritual called *"motjeko le motsamao"* (the dance and move) and this was a simple kill, wiggle and next battle tradition! It was believed that this tradition exhumed all the powers that the fallen had and their "chi" (life force/energy) went straight to Oba Ewaure the great himself so that he became even stronger and wiser for his people.

The King Shark's Dahomeanians on the other flank understood one language, and that was to mimic the face and actions of their ruler! Being famous for nodding his head before the battle began, to motion the freedom of killing, Behanzin Hossu Bowelle was an astute and loyal brand ambassador, face and epitome of "No mercy!" He understood that if a man desired to kill a "tick", he had to make sure that its mouth also died with it so that a disease wasn't born from it remains! If left unchecked, Egypt would have been like a tick and a comfortable tick didn't only breed in large numbers, it sucked everything up until the last drop and the King Shark, understood this assertion completely! His warriors killed in silence but licked the blood of all the Egyptians they slew as a sign of owning them in the afterlife!

No remorse was shown to the Egyptians and every kill that a Dahomeanian made had to be more vicious and brutal than the last one. Basically, the King Shark was the first protector of Wakanda and a pure blood royalist of the Jabari clan of the **Dahomey** Empire that all *"Amantshontsho Amnyama* (**Black Panthers**) were chosen from! **Wakanda** was the Dahomey capital that was known for its natural deposits of telluric iron that was later called vibranium and "*Umthubi Omnyama*" (**Black Panther**) was the title given to the king, who was ultimately the best fighter and warrior of the Dahomey Empire and famous capital of Wakanda!

However, as the Dahomey Empire eventually fell after the King Shark's death and a faction of them vacated their motherland, and settled in the peaceful and hidden area in the south of Africa where they eventually called themselves amaXhosa and their hidden knew kingdom was called Wakanda, in remembrance of the original capital and **Bashenga**, the King Shark's grandson was the first ruler of Wakanda kingdom! The Dahomeanians were not only brutal warriors but they could literally kick the living lights out of anyone and their king was even worse!

For a while, the Queen of Sheba's *Seleka* was winning easily as the battle progressed for days but that was because Pharaoh Maahes wanted them to gain confidence, before eventually showing them how great he was! Kane played the long game and he knew that when the war ended, he wanted to be in a position where all of his enemies were so weak and obliterated, to an extent that they would be literally be begging for his mercy! Most of Kane's opponents had made the mistake of thinking he was a proud egomaniac that was in charge of a large army, and without the numbers he would fall easily but 'boy' were they wrong! Kane learnt from a young age that everything could be bended to suit an intended purpose, or meet a desired goal at a specific, particular and favourable time frame.

If he could sacrifice 100 000 soldiers in order to win a war, Kane would do it without flinching! To him, honour wasn't just dying for an honourable cause or belief, it was actually escaping death itself. Kane believed he had been born as an albino so that he could live two lifetimes, first as a white god and the second, he would transcend to reside and occupy a black body, wherein he was to be the god of everything living and dead. So when he grew up as an outcast, he didn't not only embrace Glenda the Horrible's evil teachings and magic, he outgrew the very essence of being confined to what human beings believed was good and evil, and embarked on a new leaf where he believed he existed for one purpose and that was to rule everything! His war strategy was very effective and painful for both his people and opponents!

Since he had grown being deprived of all the pleasures that a child should have in a loving a caring home, his battle method was also based on that experience. Kane allowed his enemies to experience the very thing that everyone went to war for, the priceless feeling of winning! And when his enemies' spirits were high, convinced and confident of an inevitable win, just like his childhood, he took away that moment and everything away from them just like that, with a quick and calculated counter attack that was called "*Ukubahlekisa*"(to make them laugh and enjoy)!

This manoeuvre was so effective so much that most of his opponents died whilst drowning in the victory bubbles of mediocre conflict wins, whilst Kane had been systematically placing them in the right and favourable position for a total knockout! This counter attack was simple, the enemy would win the first few fights whilst the Egyptians would slowly push back and mislead the enemy that they were retreating, falling in huge numbers and at worst being totally outmatched until they reached the metres that were favourable for the Egyptian **carroballista, onager, scorpio** and **Egyptian chariots** to turn the tide quickly, effortlessly and effectively!

The Carroballista

While the basic ballista was created by the ancient Greeks and Africans, there is no doubt that the Egypt under Kane took this machine and adapted it for their own use on the battlefield. The *carroballista* was developed from an earlier *manuballista*. However, its distinction lay in its maneuverability. Fundamentally, the weapon was created as a truck-mounted ballista to carry versatile field weapons. The weighted springs were made of iron and had leather covers to protect them from enemy fire and the weather. To shoot, one man turned the winch to move back the slider and rope, while another held it steady and placed a bolt on the slider, allowing the first man to pull the trigger, and this weapon claimed many lives under the tactical genius of the shrewd Kane!

Onager

Kane also invented and used heavier mounted gun frameworks that could use rocks as missiles to bring down walls, small fortresses and ultimately shield walls of opposing armies. The *onager* (named after the wild ass because of its kick) was a kind of sling. It consisted of a large frame with a sling attached to the front end. The sling was used to hold projectiles that could be fired by forcing the arm of the sling down against the tension of twisted ropes or springs. The speed and distance of the projectile depended on the wind and the terrain.

Scorpio

The Scorpio or scorpion was type of ancient artillery piece which was also known by the name of the triggerfish. It was a catapult that had remarkable precision and power, and was particularly dreaded by the enemies of the Egyptian Empire. It was more of a sniper weapon than a siege engine, operated by one man and was basically an early crossbow, a "catapult with bolts", used on a larger scale by the Egyptian legions. During the Gusu war, 60 scorpio per legion was the standard, or two for every regiment. The scorpio had mainly two functions in a regiment. In precision shooting, it was a weapon of marksmanship capable of cutting down any foe within a distance of 100 meters whilst in parabolic shooting, the range was greater, with distances up to 400 meters and a firing rate that was high as (3 to 4 shots per minute). The Egyptians used the scorpio where there was artillery battery at the top of a hill or high ground where they had stationed a flank, which was protected by the main body of the main regiment. In such a scenario, the scorpio could be used to fire up to 240 bolts per minute at the enemy army and the weight and speed of the bolts were sufficient enough to pierce enemy shields, and ultimately to kill them.

Egyptian Chariot

Chariots were the first racing cars of the ancient world and were invented by Egyptians and quickly became not only the preferred mode of transport for royalty and the elite, but also revolutionized military tactics and warfare. In the hands of Kane, chariots were heavy weapons used to crash into the troops of Egyptian enemies and supporting the archers, swords and spearmen who manned them. This earliest form of military wagon had four wheels drawn by four asses or ass/onager hybrids, together with a driver and a warrior armed with spears, bow and arrows and axes riding into battle over the corpses of the slain. It was this military development that gave the real impetus to the Egyptian warfare and chariot, which was an effective weapon combining high speed, strength, durability and mobility that could not be matched by the Seleka's large infantry.

These were the weapons that turned the tide against the Queen of Sheba's seleka in favour of Pharaoh Maahes. It was a shocking a sudden counter attack that was unavoidable and at the same time unprecedented, considering that no one knew how much or what type of hidden fire power the Egyptians were going to use in such a war! It was a total knockout and everyone knew it as countless of Shebaninas, Beninians, Ethiopians, Kongonians, Dahomeanians and Abantu fell in ridiculous numbers!

No one thought it could get so good and go so bad abruptly at the same time! It got to a point that the *seleka's* warriors were being decapitated in numbers that led Ntu to negotiate a one day truce with Kane so that the Seleka could clear the battlefield and bury the piles of corpses of their loved ones, as the Egyptians were literally using their dead bodies as shield walls to evade and defend against the seleka's arrows!

It was a brutal and unrelenting war, i a no mercy battle and the loser was going to be enslaved at least and butchered at worst! The truce was called "*Umncwabo*" (the burial) to signify the burial of loved ones who had left them at an unfortunate and unprecedented time, and Kane also did the same in his camp as he buried the fallen Egyptian warriors! However life is a funny thing as one man once postulated. An advantage can suddenly turn to a disadvantage if a person relaxes to pursue the victory and this was the unfortunate and decisive moment that altered the shape of African history as Kane also found out!

During "*umncwabo*", both camps took the time to nurse the injured and reevaluate their strategies but none of the camps surprisingly foresaw an Egyptian defeat or Seleka win at this point! The seleka was ready to die a warrior's death by giving its best and jolting the last kicks of a dying horse but the arrival of the supreme Mossi Empire swayed the war to the seleka's favour and guaranteed their victory. The **Mossi Empire** wasn't involved in the war and had actually refused the Queen of Sheba's invitation to join it. However when, **Yennenga, Mogho Naba Na Nageda's** daughter was killed by Kane, as she was caught in a crossfire of the war, the Mossi Empire came swiftly and ruthlessly with a vengeful vendetta against Egypt, and they were the ones that decided the war!

The Mossi Empire

The foundation of the Mossi kingdom started from Na Negeda also called Gbewa and he was the king of the biggest portion of the empire, whilst he stationed his 3 sons as tributary kings to control other Mossi territories. Negeda also had a daughter named **Yennenga** who was celebrated for her beauty and for bringing good luck to the Mossi armies on the battlefields. She was so loved by her father that he would not let her marry.

During the Gusu war she was unprecedentedly carried away by a mad horse, and was caught in the crossfire of the war in the Egyptian camp as they were recuperating and mending the wounds of the in- jured warriors, as they awaited another tussle at dawn. Her husband was a Mande king and hunter named Rialé who upon learning that his queen had been caught in the tug of war of two unrelenting bulls, had no choice, than to seek the assistance of a man who was at first furious that he had married his beloved daughter but had accepted the marriage because Rialé provided the Mossi with horses and soldiers for their imperialist endeavours.

Na Nageda had tried to avoid the war by all means even when the Queen of Sheba had asked for his assistance he had refused because he virtually saw no gain for his people in it and besides his empire was peaceful at the time! However when the Egyptians had captured his daughter who unfortunately had apprehended herself to them practically, he had no choice but to do what any loving father would, he joined the war but as independent party and not an ally to anyone! In the region of the Niger River, the Mossi were known to go to war like lions against their enemies because they scouted their enemies for weak spots, and when it came to the chase they went for the throat and suffocate the enemy when they least expected it.

Unlike other tribes, the Mossi considered Islam and Christianity to be the mental weapons of conquest by the superior powers against the minority. They were radical African traditionalist that went above and beyond in regulating trade with neighbouring Muslim and Christian tribes with remarkable strictness. They forbad Muslims to settle in their lands and even worse, to own it! The practice of both these religions was outlawed and anyone who broke this law was either killed or castrated.

The king bore the title of *Mogho Naba Na Nageda*. "*Mogho*" meaning "the country", "the ordered space"; and "the divine law". *Naba* meant Chief or Master and like Pharaoh, Mogho Naba Na Nageda had the greatest Nam (divine energy), which enabled him to dominate evil forces and rule effectively. This higher energy was symbolized by a fire that was lit throughout his reign, a practice that was also done by the baTéké in Gabon and also found in the Zimbabwe Empire.

No one spoke to Na Nageda directly like the Mansa of Mali even if he was close family member or friend, without the royal minister being the intermediary. The King's daughter wasn't just a beloved wife, queen and daughter, she was the one who wore her father's clothes and held the office of renegade ruler if the king died for the duration of the funeral. All the nobility would bow down before her and the King's widows would shave their hair and give it to her so that she blew and blessed it as it fell on their husband's grave.

This practice was believed to be a sign of allegiance to their king even in the afterlife so that they ascertained their position in his empire in the afterlife as well! The Mossi people were experts in crossing and breeding horses and donkeys which were in demand everywhere. This meant that they were the bosses of cavalry warfare as everyone got to witness as they galloped in full stride into the war!

The Kill, End and Beginning *(Ukubulala, Lesiphetho, Lesiqalo)*

When Yennenga was captured in the Egyptian camp, Kane did the most unthinkable and inhuman thing possible. Since the Mossi were famous and gifted high jumpers he challenged the Yennenga to a game of, 'Gusimbuka Urukiramende,' which in theory was the earliest form of high jump, as a sport and entertainment. For every mistake she made she was violated by two elite officers but for every jump she breezed through she was made to drink large quantities of water, which began to flow out of her nostrils! She beat all the Egyptians eloping heights of over 2 meters. After she had won 3 straight jumps without fail, Kane decided to raise his warrior's spirit by personally challenging her to the largest jump possible but the catch was that she had to go first so that when she failed he would then kill and humiliate her either way.

It was war and soldiers grew weary of battle without proper entertainment to refresh their minds and sharpen their focus and goals for war and one of the hidden but key reason for ancient wars was unfortunately women! Women were the spoils of war and the victors could chose and plunder them as they willed. The elite were the first to choose for their royal harems and slave courtyards, and the rest was divided amongst the soldiers. Anything or anyone that wasn't Egyptian was rendered as an enemy by Kane thus it or he/she had to be subdued, accessed and killed if need be and this was the fate that awaited Na Negeda's daughter.

As intended she failed this particular jump and Kane was the first to violate her. When he was done, he sliced her open into two halves and instructed the lowest ranking soldiers to violate the *"useless chops of meat"* as he deemed it for the amusement of his high ranking officials. However when the news came to Emperor Na Negeda's door he didn't just declare war on Egypt, he wrote *"incwadi yesifungo sokufa"* (a death promise letter) to the Egyptian Pharaoh called **"Inyembezi Zomzali Kaziweliphansi!"** (The Tears of a Parent don't fall to the ground)

Inyembezi Zomzali Kaziweliphansi Letter

The letter to Kane was direct and precise and to make sure that Kane saw the type of man he was dealing with now, Emperor Na Negeda had ordered his *"inhloli"* (a royal messenger of bad news) to break his own neck after delivering the letter. This would be a more painless and honourable death compared to what death at the Egyptians' could be like, because the fact was he was a dead man either way. So when messenger barged in, the Egyptian camp and was brought forth to Pharaoh to present Emperor Na Nageda's letter, he twisted his own neck and died on the spot, much to the disbelief of the Egyptian elites that were present! Even Kane himself was a bit moved by this act and immediately ordered one of his army captains called Ananaz to read the letter loudly to him.

Ananaz: The letter reads my liege (**gulping**)….. "Kane… Kane… Kane! I have called you three times because these are the same 3 times that my daughter screamed out in pain telling you to stop but you didn't as you violated her! You think you know pain? Know the feeling of worrying about a child that will never come back, even if it's just for a moment? I never wanted this feeling or these thoughts that have made me sleepless but because you reek of evil, you have come to the light and touched and plundered what is sacred! I only promise you one thing Kane… by this time tomorrow, my daughter will be wiping her marble kitchen floors with your insides in the afterlife and dusting off her sandals on your children's dissected bosoms… Your pregnant women shall be sliced open alive and the babies shall be fed off to the Nile and then we shall see if it gives life like you believe it does! But be of good cheer for your skull shall be preserved and conserved for all generations that will dwell in these lands and beyond to see, and know that an ancient evil was trampled in these lands by the horses and sword of the Mossi! If you have received this letter then its time to kiss the cheeks and *foreheads of your loved ones goodbye because at day break tomorrow you will surely take the last gasps of breath in this world as I stand over your rotting corpse!*

When Ananaz had finished reading the letter from the Mossi king, there was dead silence in the Egyptian camp because no one had thought that they would be fighting at many fronts at the same time, and the worst part was that Egyptian soldiers were not only weary from the rigid warfare that Kane was deploying them to frequently, they knew that would not survive an inspired and fresh Mossi front at this particular time of the battle! It was simple a straight slaughter as the seleka would be coming from the other front and the Mossi from another. For the first time ever, it dawned on the Egyptians that they were not no longer the indomitable force as before, and that power is never stagnant, it moves all over from time to time and the oppressor can become the oppressed!

There was only one option and this decision was a coward's way out but it was the only way out if the Egyptians were to save themselves! Ananaz and some of the captains seeing that their king was literally going to lead not only them to their death but probably lead to the extinction of the entire Egyptians, plotted against their Pharaoh at night! The mutual agreement was that Kane was not a true blood Egyptian and his greed for power had made him crazy and dangerous to Egypt as well as their enemies, therefore he was "expendable!"

So the plan was to wait for him to go into his sacrament chambers were he conducted his magical concoctions that he drank every day and believed to make him strong and undisputable! When he drank this, usually he fell into a long slumber that lasted some hours before waking up rejuvenated, clever and strong as ever just as Glenda the Horrible had taught him! Unfortunately for him, he couldn't cast spells like Glenda because his royal gene was believed to rebuke that element and capability but he knew the basics to heal and strengthen himself using particular herbs and tree leaves!

When he was deep in slumber, Ananaz and the other captains would tie him up on a chariot, alongside the body of messenger with *"incwadi yoxolo*[97] and set the chariot's course to Mossi territory with the hope that the Mossi Emperor was going to spare their lives! However Kane had a secret circle of spies that he kept hidden and personal to himself in the form of women slaves! He knew that slaves were not regarded as harmful in the Egyptian Empire, unlike in the Bhanda Empire, therefore great men usually disclosed confidential secrets and information carelessly without the possible thoughts of regret or probability of the secrets coming out! So when Ananaz and the other captains were plotting against him in the comfort of their gimps (sex slaves), Kane got hold of their plan as if he was there in the room himself.

His plan was simple, he was going to play along and act like he was drinking the concoction and lay in his bed asleep, such that Ananaz and his compatriots would think their plan was working! When they got inside to tie him up in his sacramental chamber, he would have his most loyal and best soldiers ready to pounce on them and tie them up instead! When they had been tied up, he was going to cut off their tongues and throw them to his pet lions, as they watched them gobble their tongues up in a single motion! After that, he was going to actually grant them the pleasure of seeing how angry the Mossi king was, by sending them as a gift and message to Na Nageda, tied to a chariot with

97 A letter of apology

the corpse of *inhloli* as they had planned to do with their own Pharaoh!

This was the birth of the saying, *"two can play the* game, as not only did the Mossi king kill them when he got them, as a reply package from Kane. He specifically followed the instructions from Kane's mockery letter called *"izipho zasebusuku*[98]*"* where he also placed the biggest sledgehammer that he could find for the Mossi king to relieve some of the tension and his stress on! The letter was basically narrating how Kane had spent the last moments with the Mossi king's daughter, and how she cried when he violated and sliced her into two for his boys to enjoy themselves!

However the biggest detail on that letter were highlighted in bold and informed the Mossi king, to use the sledge hammer that came with the chariot as he saw fit on the "gift" that came with the body of his royal messenger! When Na Nageda was finished and tired after breaking bones and skulls and creating mincemeat out of his "gift" he stayed all night, making sure that every Mossi warriors got a chunk of braai-ed Egyptian meat, before the war at dawn! This was believed to not only seal their victory against the Egyptians but make the Mossi stronger physically and mentally! So when dawn finally broke loose, the Mossi came flying against the Egyptians in all directions!

Some died without even removing the sleeping bags from their eyes because the Mossi had come at them very early, quick and suddenly at their own camp before they had even dreamt of breakfast! As the Egyptians got into their battle formations and lines, the Mossi were picking them off in numbers. It was a clever idea from Na Nageda to bring the war to them as early and possible and it was proving to work outstandingly! On the other side, at the Queen of Sheba's *seleka*'s camp, the alli-

98 The gifts of the night

ance woke up to battle screams and the teeth gnashing sound of metal, slashing against metal as the Egyptians and Mossi battalions battled it out on the other side of the camp!

At first *Dagaalyahanada xorriyadda* seleka quickly took arms thinking that the Egyptians had snooped under their watch and attacked them in their camp, since the camps were close, and the sound from the battle at the Egyptian camp, could be heard as clear and loud as if it was inside the seleka's camp!

When *Dagaalyahanada xorriyadda seleka* leaders saw that it was a fight from the other camp, they assumed that a civil war or some sought of disaccord had arose within the Egyptian camp, therefore they were fighting about! Whatever the situation was, this was the opportunity that the *seleka* needed to go all in against the Egyptians, whilst they were presumably disco-ordinated and unfocused. So without anything to lose or left to ponder over, the *seleka* attacked the Egyptians from the front side of both camps, where the previous battle had been fought, whilst the Mossi had attacked them from the rear because it was nearer to their territory! For hours, the armies battled it with the Egyptian head count dwindling in astronomical figures!

It was like for every alliance or Mossi warrior that fell, five more Egyptians fell in response. The Mossi and the *seleka* were solo projects although they had a shared understanding of defeating a mutual enemy. Just as Na Nageda had promised, all the Egyptians were killed except Kane himself and a prisoner that he had held bound since his forced ascension to the Egyptian throne! When they unmasked the Egyptian prisoner, no one could tell who he was but only that he had the foul stench of a man who had gone months without a bath, and his hair was long and all over the place with scruffiness. Kane was vulnerable, tired and defeated! It was like Nazaar was there personally to remind him of the words he told him before he died!

Everyone wanted to kill him first but the Queen of Sheba with backing of the most feared fighter after Nazaar, "The king Shark" challenged anyone to a 2 on 2 battle if they wanted to kill Kane before she had said her peace! No one dared to even scratch their cheek in response to this open challenge because they knew what the protector of Wakanda was capable of alone! Without any further opposition besides the raised hand of Na Nageda who also wanted the same platform after the Queen of Sheba had made her speech!

Queen of Sheba:	Look at them... don't hide in your shame... take a long look at them! I told you that they shall hang your insides and celebrate by plucking out your fingers, one by one and break the skulls of your men and children and raid your wives as you watch the fruits of your own mouth lay your Empire to waste, because you blasphemed against these men's gods and brought conflict in their peaceful lands as you have mine! Today the fallen are avenged and the victors are going to sleep in peace as every men and women here today shall go home with the comforting site of your death, as you have butchered thousands of their kinsmen! Asno one is beyond forgiveness in the Lord's kingdom, seek and accept him as your Lord, Savior and King in your last moments of life and you shall be saved!
The Crowd:	Kill him... Murderer... Anarchist... Kill him, kill

him…Kill him!!! *(Chanting)*

King Na Nageda: Quiet! *(Shushing everybody with piercing stern look),* It is my turn to speak and everybody quiet! You chant coercing us to kill this dog and dear brethren rest assured that this "thing" they worshiped and believed in as Pharaoh, shall not see the end of day today! For all that don't know, this men owes me a life for my daughter's death! He violated and then killed her in the most gruesome way possible, my child, my girl, my princess… *(Sobbing)*! His life only won't suffice the pain and change what he has caused to my Empire and family dear brothers, and sisters! I evoke the right to *'ukuchitha isizwe seGibhithe' (destroy Egypt)* if all protocol present and observed agrees! These people have troubled and trampled over our lands for years, and today they should stand accountable and face our wrath and edge of the blade as we toss their loved ones into the jaws of the crocodiles in the Nile!

The Crowd: Lets kill them all… All of them… Kill… kill… kill… kill! *(Chanting)*.

King Oba Ewuare
the Great: Silence!… *"Ukuthula ebandleni"!*[99] For ven-

99 Quietness befall thee all!

189

geance I released my Beninian hordes in their full might, although many did fall to the enemy as we have all lost loved ones to this evil man that lays injured and defeated before us! Did you all hear his head count? This man killed over a 1000 of us in this war and for every 10 he killed, he marked that trophy with a tattoo of an assegai in his back! Now I ask you dear brothers and sisters, if we are to remove this man's armour, and count his overall head count on his back, don't you think he has wiped out tens and hundreds of villages alone? We may take our time and digest whatever makes us feel better and good about ourselves dear brethren but the truth of the matter is that, we are all weak and cowards for every minute and breath of air that this evil man still takes as we stand doing nothing, whilst the blood of our fallen still flows freshly on the ground, he pissed and killed them on! I repeat again, I came here for vengeance and I shall live here after the debt has been paid!

King Ezana Axum: I am of the idea that indeed this man stands to be judged and sentenced to whatever punishment is due but if I may ask! What do we hope for and after killing him, for indeed he has brought nothing but calamities and lamentations in all the lands? Because if we kill this man without a tangible answer to what we hope to achieve after killing him, then we are nothing more than the savages and barbarians that we curse ourselves! We can enslave him for life and teach him the Christian ways and walks of life whilst he seeks solace and faces retribution in exile! Our greatest weakness as Africans has always been that we are quick and swift to execute without finding reason and other possible solution, and then we later regret our deeds when a newer and stronger form of evil arises to terrorize us again! Peace be unto you all dear brothers and sisters!

Ethiopians: Peace be unto you all brothers and sisters! *(Speaking in one accord)*

King Mvemba Zinga: Kill or not to be killed, who are we? Sons and daughters of the Most High God that seek to execute the offices of the Most High? Revenge is for God my friends but sometimes a cancer is only a cancer until it is cut out from the body, and the human being begins to heal and be healthy again! If we enslave this fool King Ezana, and he escapes don't you think it would be only a matter of time before we receive heads of each other in garment wraps, as he kills each and every one of us one by one? A clever man once said when one has the advantage, always seize the moment with both hands and capitalize on it! I second King Oba on this one, such man never change and only the sword they worship is their salvation, so who are we to deny him the death that he solemnly de-serves dear brother! I second…Death!

The King Shark:	***Akafe!*[100] (Nodding his head to motion death)**
King Ntu:	I was born when the Bhanda Empire was ex-ploding and burning in large flames, as this man here stood laughing as he ordered his men to vio-late my mother and kill my father! Every year I trained and lived for one single purpose, not to be king and definitely not be in such a conversation about the life of a man, who took my childhood away from me! I have lived for more than 20 years too look straight into the eyes of this man as I run my blade through his heart and watch him bleed and squirm in pain, as I run my blade through him again and again until I even escort his evil soul to the afterlife to kill it also! So brethren if it is a question of death that you all need a vote for or against, let me save you all the hardships by volunteering to kill this man right now!

When the Queen of Sheba and King Ezana saw that there was no turning back in form of Kane's punishment, they looked at the back and realised the smelly and hairy slave was still tied up, so they ordered some of their warriors to pour water on him and gestured for him to speak if he had any words before his death also!

100 He must die

192

Prince Hor-Aha: I am Prince Hor-Aha, Son of King Narmer, a
true blood Egyptian man and today whether you
kill me or spare my life, you have saved me either
way dear people! When this men arrived as a lost
and alien orphan in Egypt, I told my father that
he would be the death of us but he never listened
to me because he came with a pride of lions following him, something that no one had seen or
done before! For years we grew up together and
with time I began to love him as my own blood
brother! We trained together and sometimes we
even ate from the same plate because we didn't
want anyone to separate us! He was the best in
everything and beat us all in whatever we thought
we were dominant in!

When my father died, my brother, my best
friend... this thing, staged a *coup de tat* to rule a
throne that was mine by birth right, and impris-
oned me whilst killing all my family so that our
dynasty was washed away! My sons, wives and
daughters, people that loved him as an uncle and
family... he killed them all mercilessly! And now
you free me, talking about death yet you see that
grief and pain has already had its way with me!
Please I beg of you! Kill me dear brothers and
sisters, that way you would have freed me of my
grief but if I have found favour in your sight then

please allow me to seek forgiveness, for the little ones and mothers that have done you no harm and have lived in peace in the stress of Egypt! You can kills us if you may but please, I only seek mercy for what's left of my people, they have been misled and misguided by a greedy leader that has led them astray!

King Shark: I have never spoken or listened to Egyptians speaking much because all they do is kill and deceive but I have never met a man who only seeks mercy for other people and not himself! I king Behanzin Hossu Bowelle, first protector of Wakanda solemnly swear to never raise my hand against you nor will any of my people Prince Hor-Aha of Egypt!

Prince Hor-Aha: Thank You Honourable King!

King Ezana Axum: I swear also!

King Mvemba Nzinga: No son of a King should go through what you have gone through! I swear also!

Queen of Sheba: I swear!

King Ntu: Death to every Egyptian! These dogs burned and killed our people alive and now they seek pardon!

No dear brethren, a man reaps what he sows and this frail and pale Prince deserve nothing more than a gruesome death as well! I vote for his death as well!

King Na Nageda: All of them should die and after that we must take over Egypt, kill everything that breathes and walks there and divide it amongst ourselves!

Queen of Sheba: This man wronged none of us here, maybe if he had been king in the first place we wouldn't even have gone to war against Egypt, King Ntu! The man that killed your parents is there! The man that killed your daughter King Na Nageda is also there! How many more innocent lives shall we plunder for the blunder of one man? Let us make a pact today and let it be known, that who so ever kills this man present today shall suffer the same fate!

Every leader eventually agreed to this pact even though it was discomforting for king Ntu and Na Nageda, due to the implication of refusing the pact and a pact, made between ancient leaders was a lifetime covenant that was to be respected and observed until the end of days! So when the tribe leaders had come to the final conclusion that Prince Hor-Aha, was to be set free and escorted back to Egypt where he reclaimed his birth right, and ruled Egypt as the rightful Pharaoh and did great wonders as his father Narmer also did. Kane on the other hand was given the podium to speak as they spate on him and kicked him

195

before he eventual got in front of them, injured and covered in blood, mucus and saliva!

Each tribe leader was holding a dagger that they were going to use to stab him with after he had said his last words, and Kane knew very well that this was it hence he made it easy for them by removing his armour and clothes!

King Ntu:	Any Last words?
Kane:	Behold, I go now! I have fought a good fight and killed the best there was and still I go now! You will kill me today but another has already been born who brings upon more terror, in a way that you have never seen before! This new born, will come with breathtaking stories, spices and promises of a great and mutual understanding of foreign lands, through trade with your lands but he will not only rule you! He will take away your lands, and his children will scatter you above and beyond, until you have no identity of your own! **(Scramble for Africa).** I die without regret for I lived the way I desired, and now I go out in a true warrior's way! But rest assured that vanity is vanity and all is vanity!

Just as they were about to swing their daggers to stab him, Kane began to whistle and speak in a scary and wild language, that evoked movement from the nearby bush. The movement made everyone alert and get into battle formations. Whatever was coming was something big and it was coming in huge numbers causing vibrations on the ground... Just as every warrior stood ready for whatever came through the bushes, a large pride of lions came out led by Simba, who roared the fiercest of them all. It wasn't a roar for war or any form of hunt or attack! It was simply a goodbye between two friends, 'the king of Africa and the king of the jungle!'"

All the lions roared after Simba had finished his roar and everyone stood there mortified at this spectacle, until Kane told them that it was time, he was ready! One by one they stabbed him and he never made a sound but only shed a tear that mirrored Simba's roar until he fell dead on the ground, and Simba stopped roaring as well! It was like a high intensity scene of a sad story and yet everyone didn't know how to feel about themselves or what had just transpired t!

Killing this man had been the hardest thing that anyone could do but even after death, it seemed he had a hold over a lot of people's lives! The lions followed Simba as he galloped straight to the dead corpse of Maahes, their King's brother and friend! Simba then made one defeaning roar that seemed more of a cry and more of a howl than roar of pain!

As everyone stood watching, the lions then began to devour Kane's body after Simba had finished roaring until nothing was left, much to the disbelief and shock of everyone that stood there watching! Kane was known as the god of lions and a lion himself, and this was the way that his lion family buried him, as an honour to his greatness and stature amongst them!

It might have been viewed as a terrible way to go by most but even in death, Kane didn't give his enemies the pleasure to dishonour and humiliate his legacy! Yes they killed him and he fell like all men do but to the lions, he was a god and he roared just like them! No one got his remains or kept a trophy of what was left of him. The lions simple wiped out his very existence on the face of the earth!

Without any vendetta, agenda or mutual interest keeping the tribes stationed in **Shum Laka**, everyone went their separate ways back to their lands astonished and mortified at what had happened as it was more than the victory itself!

These are the **Stories of An Ancient African Civilization,** that have been lost to history or worst, told as bed time stories, to generations that do not know where it all began, or who they owe their freedom and ethnicity to!

ACKNOWLEGDEMENTS

I BLAME ALL of YOU that inspired and encouraged me to write this book. Although I would like to take this opportunity to thank and appreciate you, this has been a testing exercise in suistained agony. Hence,to all that played a large role in prolonging my agonies with your encouragement and support,well …you know who you are and you owe me and I will collect! To the readers, you guys rock and it's a blessing that you have stuck with me through this epic roller coaster of a saga, through cliff hangers, anxiety and feels. I wouldn't trade you for all the glitter in the world, THANK YOU!

www.ingramcontent.com/pod-product-compliance
Lightning Source LLC
Chambersburg PA
CBHW052041090426
42739CB00010B/1993